a

Penning the Pandemic

EXECUTIVE EDITOR
Carl Mabbs-Zeno

ASSOCIATE EDITORS
Rodger Martin
Maura MacNeil
Ronnie McIntire
Jesseca Timmons

Penning the Pandemic was produced through cooperation between the Monadnock Writers' Group and Khotso Publishing. Unless otherwise noted: images are from the UK National Archives and portray the London plague of 1665.

ISBN 978-1-7331262-5-0

Khotso Publishing
Peterborough, NH
2020

Table of Contents

POETRY

SHORT STORIES

THEATER

Introduction

On this, all of humanity can agree, the first half of 2020 has been extraordinary. We have adjusted our manners of living in ways that six months before were conceivable only in fiction. These adjustments and the COVID-19 virus itself have affected so many people profoundly through personal tragedy or humane sympathy. This pandemic is a unique, memorable experience in the lives of all living generations.

For the past six months, the American news media covered the pandemic with remarkable tenacity – offering a flow of medical, epidemiological, economic, and political analyses and speculation. In contrast, this volume collects impressions formed by creative writers. With a diverse palette of literary styles and genres, ranging from memoir to poetry to short story to theater, these writers express emotions, experiences, fears, ironies and humor. In a time of isolation, reading these various approaches on the shared crisis draws us closer through the familiarity of the human voice.

June 29, 2020

Plague and Pandemic in Classic Literature

English Plague - 1361

For God is deaf nowadays and deigneth not us to hear that girls for their guilts he forgrint [destroys] them all.

William Langland, *Piers Plowman*

London Plague – 1606

The dead man's knell is there scarce asked for who, and good men's lives expire before the flowers in their caps dying or ere they sicken.

Shakespeare, *Macbeth*, Act 4, Scene 3

London Plague – 1665-66

Lord! How sad a sight it is to see the streets empty of people.

Samuel Pepys, *Diary*

My friend Dr. Heath was of opinion that it might be known by the smell of their breath: but then, as he said, who durst smell to that breath for his information? since, to know it, he must draw the stench of the plague up into his own brain, in order to distinguish the smell!

Daniel Defoe, *A Journal of the Plague Year*, 1722

I think it ought to be recorded to the honour of such men, as well as clergy, surgeons, apothecaries, magistrates, and officers of every kind, as also all useful people who ventured their lives in discharge of their duty, as most certainly all such as stayed did up to the last degree, and served all these kinds did not only venture but lose their lives on that sad occasion.

Daniel Defoe, *A Journal of the Plague Year*, 1722

He dreamed that the whole world was condemned to a terrible new strange plague that had come to Europe from the depths of Asia.

Fyodor Dostoyevsky, *Crime and Punishment*, 1866

Nobel Prize winners

> And I know, too, that we must keep endless watch on ourselves lest in a careless moment we breathe in somebody's face and fasten the infection on him. What's natural is the microbe. All the rest – health, integrity, purity (if you like) – is a product of the human will, of a vigilance that must never falter.
>
> Albert Camus, *The Plague*, 1947

> He knew what those jubilant crowds did not know but could have learned from books: that the plague bacillus never dies or disappears for good; that it can lie dormant for years and years in furniture and linen-chests; that it

bides its time in bedrooms, cellars, trunks and bookshelves; and that perhaps the day would come when, for the bane and the enlightening of men, it roused up its rats again and sent them forth to die in a happy city.

Albert Camus, final words in *The Plague*

We came out of internment only three days ago, Ah, you were in quarantine, Yes, Was it hard, Worse than that, How horrible, You are a writer, you have, as you said a moment ago, an obligation to know words, therefore you know that adjectives are of no use to us, if a person kills another, for example, it would be better to state this fact openly, directly, and to trust that the horror of the act, in itself, is so shocking that there is no need for us to say it was horrible, Do you mean that we have more words than we need, I mean that we have too few feelings, or that we have them but have ceased to use the words they express, And so we lose them.

Jose Saramago, *Blindness* 1995

Fear, like the thought of dying, makes us feel alone, but the recognition that we are all experiencing a similar anguish draws us out of our loneliness.

Orhan Pamuk, "What Plague Novels Tell Us," *New York Times*, April 26, 2020

Personal Experiences

Containers

Sarah Franklin

For as long as I can remember, one whole wall in my father's garage contained shelves of empty glass jars. Rows of every shape and size, no longer holding pickled, sauced, jellied, cukes, tomatoes, peaches, or whatever type of food they were used for. All sat there waiting for their next assignment from their captain who didn't want to waste a thing. The stacks of egg boxes, styrofoam containers, milk cartons and paper towel rolls all lived in an orderly fashion on another shelf waiting to be handy too. I always knew my dad was a child of the depression, but I never really understood it until now. I guess when your main reason for being is to survive, an instinctual part of yourself emerges. Rationing, reusing, recreating uses for everyday things, become the norm out of necessity. One's habits don't go away. As my father said, "you never know when you may need it," referring to an old candle stub or an empty Clorox jug which he would stash with the others he had somewhere in the house. I always thought he went a bit overboard with his saving of things. Now, as I try to protect and feed my family without any money coming in, I understand my father more than I ever have. He is right here with me at this Covid-19 time.

As a child I would accompany my father every Saturday to the A & P to do the weekly grocery shopping. I used to love to see the new products each week; like strawberry ice cream sauce in a plastic squeeze container or Fluff that came in a wide mouth jar. Often he'd let me throw one of these new-fangled products into our cart, (maybe just because he liked the shape of the container), and often I'd get home and find out it was disgusting. The best part of this weekly journey was the ritual at checkout of picking out an Oh Henry! Payday, or 10,000 Dollar Bar. He would give me my 50-cent allowance that day too, so it was a double whammy. Having my father's quiet attention for those few hours each week fueled me. He was a man of very few words but his actions spoke love and I felt it walking down those aisles jam-packed with cans and jars that he picked wisely; and me, frivolously.

My father loved to cook for masses of people. Feeding others gave him pleasure. Ham and bean suppers for a whole church congregation, 35 grilled chickens over a big barbecue pit for our family reunions, gourmet dinners in the middle of Labrador on his canoe expeditions. It didn't matter where he was, the planning, prepping and execution of meals were rewarded by watching the recipients scoffing them down together. When there isn't much food, the sharing of it becomes sacred. Our evening meal, now, has become the one time we connect as a family during the day. Coming from our separate territories within our house, we light the candle and send our thoughts to someone in need or pain and "dig in" as my father used to say.

My father worked two jobs when he put himself through law school. One was at a paper manufacturer, night shift. He used to take naps on great big soft rolls while the other workers covered for him. I remember my father joking about my mother having "toiletpaperphobia" (all one word), which he said quickly to make it sound like a real ailment. She was afraid to run out of toilet paper, he finally explained to me when I didn't get the joke. Now I also get an extra 12 rolls every time I don my mask and gloves and go shopping. You never know when they might run out.

Every spring my father would take the milk cartons he had collected over the winter, cut the tops off, fill the bottom half with homemade compost and start his vegetable seeds. When he got home from the office every day you could find him in the garden weeding, planting and tending to the bounty that would come later and feed us throughout the fall. When I realized we may be in self isolation for a long while, with worries of hunger and world famine, I got my seeds ready. I've filled my empty egg cartons with compost to start tomatoes, broccoli, and greens. Old file cabinet drawers have become garden beds with potatoes, kale and cauliflower. I will spend my afternoons cultivating the vision of my family eating the rewards of my labor.

My father and I used to take long walks in the woods together. There were never very many words exchanged. We were both happy to enjoy just the sights, sounds and each other's presence. The only thing he would say now and then was "take in a deep breath." We would fill our lungs together drinking in the clean air and serenity of the forest.

I never knew my father was teaching me how to survive until now. His idiosyncratic ways were just who he was. I guess when you survive a depression you come out the other side changed. You have experienced something unprecedented and you can never go back. He used to say the only thing that matters is love. His came from his actions. Each of his empty jars and containers were filled with it. Thus, so are mine.

Together Apart Again

Valerie Carter

Nothing much is pulling my attention away from the Covid 19 updates on the morning news these days, but this morning my husband's rapid knee bouncing in my peripheral vision is accomplishing that task. I've seen his hyper leg movement on multiple occasions, but I've only seen his overall countenance appear this way once before.

Seven years ago, he had arrived in Kansas City on his flight from Boston as he had done every three weeks or so for the previous eleven years. His schedule with the Cambridge, MA fire department allowed us to maintain that frequency of seeing one another during our long-distance relationship and marriage at that point. We only had four more years to manage what we called being "together apart", before my son would graduate from high school and either go off to college or move with me to the Northeast if he chose. We looked forward to the day when we could remove the word apart from "together apart," and simply be together.

That Friday, April 19th, 2013, he sat staring at the TV screen, leg bouncing rapidly, muscles tense, and distress visible on every feature of his face. I had been watching too but had a different mix of emotions stirring inside.

I was grateful that he wasn't amidst the bullet-proof vested, gun-wielding scene being televised from Watertown, MA as it unfolded. Being the Tactical Medic Team Commander as part of the Cambridge Police Special Response Team, he would have been there. He was the one who had created, formed, trained, and deployed the Tactical Medic Team. This was the first, and possibly only, big event that his team would be involved in. He wanted to be there.

I had felt both guilty and grateful as I sat next to him moving my head back and forth between him and the drama on TV. His arms were crossed, his knee was bouncing, and his head was shaking as he muttered curse words at the fact that he wasn't there with his team as they helped search for the remaining Boston Marathon bombing suspect.

So, on this rainy April morning, seven years later, in our now New Hampshire home as the news program talks about the Covid 19 situation in hospitals, I watch as my paramedic husband shakes his head and bounces his knee to try and dissipate the stress that is mounting within him. He reaches for another tissue to catch his next sneeze.

Something in the air causes him to experience sinus issues and congestion nearly every spring, and he is usually able to work right on through, but this is no ordinary spring of course. Although he tested negative for the Coronavirus, due to current circumstances, he is being required to take the next week off from his work as a paramedic in the emergency room at Lawrence General Hospital. Those are the rules.

We haven't slept in the same room since early February and continue to remain a safe distance apart within our home due to his repeated potential exposure to the virus. No sitting next to one another, no hand holding, no hugging, and most certainly no kisses. In the beginning I had joked with him saying, "This shouldn't be a problem. We trained for this for fourteen years." As the months roll by, it has become more burdensome for us both. Even when we lived 1500 miles apart, we touched more frequently than we do now while living under the same roof.

As he sits there watching the coverage about hospital workers on the news this morning, he once again feels like he is missing out on being able to play his important role within the system during a time of crisis. I share compassion for his situation and try to comfort him with the knowledge that he will only be out for five more days, and the pandemic will most likely still be in full swing when he returns to work. He reaches for another tissue and nods as his head falls backward, mouth open in anticipation of his next sneeze. "AH...choo!" The finale noise of his sneeze is muffled in the tissue. "I know. You're right." His knee doesn't seem to agree yet.

I pick up the remote control and offer up a question. "Perhaps we should turn this off. What do you think?"

"I think that might be wise." The bouncing leg slows.

In the past, I might have gone over to kiss his forehead, or rub his shoulders, but that would violate our current safety rules. Instead we just lock eyes across the room and smile.

Although it is a new, and unwelcome type of "together apart," it is one that I know we can handle. Love found a way to guide us through the changing obstacles within our long-term, long-distance relationship for fourteen years, and I am certain that it will continue to do the same for us now.

Quiet Water Flowing

Volkert Volkersz

The brakes were applied to my life on Friday, March 13. This loud, fast-moving train hissed and squealed, gradually slowing down and then things got quiet. As news of the COVID-19 pandemic became real for the Monadnock Region, I found myself cancelling events at the community center where I am the program coordinator, first for two weeks, then for a month, and finally indefinitely. Then my upcoming gigs as a folk singer got cancelled. And finally my church, where I sing in the choir, got cancelled.

As we learned more about the coronavirus, my wife and I decided to make some changes to maintain our health. To boost our immune systems, we increased our intake of Vitamin C and probiotics. And then we decided we would walk, weather permitting, every day, which would not only give us exercise and fill our lungs with fresh air, but would increase our exposure to natural Vitamin D from the sun.

With no need to go places in the car, except for quick visits to the nearby grocery store, I had more time on my hands to read. I looked at my shelves, and was drawn to books by monks from various monastic traditions. I figured this was a good time to learn something from people who were comfortable being alone with silence and solitude.

I picked up a volume by Thich Nhat Hanh, the Vietnamese Zen Buddhist master who is known for his teachings on mindfulness. Mindful breathing is at the heart of his teaching: sitting in silence for short periods of time and focusing on the in and out your breath. He also emphasizes mindful walking, focusing on each step, as well as cultivating compassion for people, animals, plants and minerals.

Then I turned to Metropolitan Hierotheos Vlachos, who writes from the Greek Orthodox monastic tradition as practiced on the holy mountain, Mount Athos, in Greece. He focuses on hesychia (or stillness), eliminating distractions, and on practicing prayer of the heart.

The third author I went to was Thomas Merton, the well-known Roman Catholic monk, poet, author and peace activist. Merton writes about the interior, the silent, the contemplative, listening. All three authors stress the importance of quietness, inner peace, attentiveness, and meditation or prayer in the here and now.

My wife and I are fortunate to live in a part of Peterborough with access to several trails not far from our front door which we have enjoyed for many years. After the pandemic hit, we decided to explore a trail we had not gone down before. After a pleasant walk along our country road and then into the woods, we found ourselves at a spot overlooking a beaver pond, with water rushing over a beaver dam and continuing down the river. Thrilled with our discovery, we sat on a couple large granite rocks, soaking up some early spring sun, listening to the quiet roar of the small waterfall, and watching ducks and Canada geese on the pond.

The next day we returned with water bottles and trail mix, determined to stay longer. My wife brought a book and I brought along my small Backpacker guitar. We had this small quiet peninsula to ourselves. We chose two different spots so as not to distract each other. I sat for a time listening to the sounds of the water going over the beaver dam. There were musical pitches resonating in the ripples and bubbles. Then I pulled out my small guitar to play along with the drone of the waterfall.

My Backpacker was tuned in DADGAD. That's a unique tuning that gives the guitar a harp-like quality with melodic tones able to ring out and sustain. As I sat in Creation, with the waterfall creating an ison, or drone-like quality, I found myself quietly playing the Protestant hymn, "This Is My Father's World." As I played the hymn over and over again, like a carillon in a church tower, a pair of ducks swam near and listened. A short while later a beaver paddled across the pond, returning to its nearby lodge. My music was harmonizing with the natural world. With my breath and my mind, my fingers and ears, I found myself entering into a meditative state.

I began to improvise a melody, imagining that this was my private Zen garden. My guitar started to sound like a Japanese koto, with notes plucked and bending, and staying close to the pentatonic (5 tone) scale. I'm not sure how long I played, maybe an hour. At one point I thought I needed to record this, so I could remember it and relive it later on. I pulled out my iPhone, started a voice memo, and recorded my newly evolving piece of meditative music. When my wife emerged from her reading spot, she commented on the Asian quality of what she heard.

For the next several weeks, this new piece of music was all I wanted to play on my guitar. Each time it brought me back, not only to that peaceful place by the pond, but to that prayerful state of mind that I found there. My music, during this time of solitude, had found a new center. I didn't need to play for an audience. I didn't need applause. I was happy that my wife heard it, and liked it, but I was playing it mainly for my Creator, and for his Creation. I found myself connecting with something deeper, something in my heart that also connected with the natural world around me.

A few days after creating this new guitar piece, I went back to the beaver pond alone. On my walk back home, I did some exploring and discovered other trails in the woods that would enable us to make the trek going through the woods and avoiding the road. It would take a bit longer, but there would be no cars.

Over the course of this quarantine (more than two months now) we have walked these trails through the woods to our quiet place almost daily. We have seen Spring come alive. Bare beech and maple trees have budded forth in their greenery. The ducks and geese have been joined by turtles, a water snake that swims by almost every time we're there, and a muskrat that enjoys paddling across the pond. We heard the frogs singing their glorious symphony at the beginning of mating season, and for a few days, we got to see them in action, splashing in the water. We have seen fish jumping, and water bugs darting around. With the warm May weather, we've also experienced the black flies and mosquitos. We've sat on our rocks in the comfortable sunshine, and on chilly days when it felt like it might snow again. We've felt the wind coming out of the north, making waves and singing its whirling song. On other days, the pond was still and clear as a mirror, reflecting the trees, tall grass and cattails on the other shore.

Sometimes I take my little Backpacker and play my Zen-like piece. Sometimes I bring a book. Most times I just sit and pray and breathe and meditate and listen to the voices of Nature and try to be attentive to my surroundings.

A month after I began composing my new music, I played it for the virtual open mic that I host for our community center. My friends enjoyed the piece, and one of them asked for its title. I had to answer that it didn't have a name yet. After thinking about it overnight, I emailed my friend the next day and wrote, it's called "Quiet Water Flowing."

And I even thought of a haiku to go with the music:

Breathing in and out
Quiet water flowing down
Ison to my song.

COVID Constraints

Irene Kreissle

As I was describing my nursing home visits to my 97-year-old mother, my friend remarked "that's what they do in jail." She meant it as a joke, but I thought about it and could see some truth to how this virus has jailed us all, especially the elderly. Now when I visit her, the nursing home staff wheel her up to a glass exterior door. I sit on the outside with my cell phone, she sits on the inside with the nursing home phone. Though she has dementia, most days when we do this she does understand that and why I can't come in and our conversations flow easily. She usually asks about family, and often makes the comparison between what is happening now with COVID 19 to what happened with the polio virus after "the war." But there have been harder days when she cries because I can't go in – not understanding. Sometimes she simply does not understand that I am on the other end of the phone, not comprehending why I would call her if I am right in front of her. Again, some days she gets it, and some days she does not. Though I suppose that her just being able to see me and I her is a blessing, I do not always feel blessed. Sometimes I am downright angry at a virus that shamelessly steals from my mother the one thing she so desperately needs – human contact – in an effort to keep her safe and alive. I wonder, if at least for my mother's sake, if it would not be better if I could go in and hug her – even if she were to contract the disease from me. It is in these times that I wish I could magically slip through the window, hug her and tell her that it will be O.K.; but of course I can't, and here it is I that am held hostage by the virus. I know that I can try again next week and perhaps then her mind will allow her to understand. My mother is just one of thousands of elderly in our country "jailed" by the virus, and I know that at this point many have stopped trying to visit as "outside the window" visits can be so hard. I, however, believe that any time I can spend with my Mother is precious and I will take it and hold on to it despite the virus' current "jailing" parameters.

Hunter/Gatherers

Mona Anderson

The night before I cancel my life, I have dinner with two friends at a local restaurant. It's March 12, so we talk about the coronavirus but mostly about our families, our lives. We share some unease in meeting at all, laughing at our elbow bumps, but still believing we can control our safety. I call it The Last Supper. The next morning I'm grounded. A few days later, everyone is.

Now my husband and I voraciously consume the covid news. I crave solid information, but it changes every hour. I watch a video on how to decontaminate packages after going to the store. I read an article that tells me I don't have to do that. The confusion confuses me. I have an unfamiliar knot in my stomach that feels like indigestion.

We live in the country and have always kept a well-stocked pantry since a trip to the grocery store is at least an hour out of the day. Yet, like everyone else, we wonder how long our food will last, and being in the elderly high-risk group, what our risk will be in shopping. We hurtle from food on the periphery of our lives to food obsession.

We discuss it for hours, for days. Where to go, when, what we need, what can we do without, will they have toilet paper, do we really need yeast, how can we be safe? Finally, twelve days into our confinement, we timidly venture out. Our usual grocery store has "senior" hours from 6 to 7, and it snowed last night so maybe we'll be one of the brave few.

We wear ventilator masks from my husband's woodworking shop. We look like Darth Vader's poor cousins.

"I'm embarrassed," I tell my husband, although no one in the store, which turns out to be surprisingly full instead of empty, seems to notice or care. I suspect other shoppers go home, though, and say to friends and family, 'You should have seen this crazy couple in the grocery store today.'

"We're safer this way," he replies, and I can't disagree.

Not a single other person wears any kind of mask, nor keeps a six-foot distance. The knot of indigestion grows.

Our primary target is milk, and it's one of the few shelves not decimated. Still, when we get to the check out, we're told we can only have two. We feel defeated and discouraged, but the pantry, at least, will be replenished.

At home, we wipe down everything with Lysol wipes, wash our hands, and strip off our clothes and jackets and put them in the washing machine. It doesn't seem like enough if the virus really is on anything, but it makes us feel better.

The next day our son begs us to stay home and let him know if we needed anything. But how can we ask him to risk his own health for us? We continue to obsess, a focus on food that feels like an unconscious ancestral, primal, need for survival. We hunt and gather our food in grocery stores but we won't go in now, and we don't want our son to go. We hunt for alternatives.

I try to breathe. The morning sun offers a clear sky with crisp, clean air. The southern horizon is almost white and deepens into a vast ocean azure in the north. The bare trees stand strong and unyielding. I feel the silence in what is. Clean air. Okay, I can breathe.

And still we obsess about food. We have enough. But...will we when... When what?

We walk down the road to buy eggs from our neighbor's egg stand. Two dozen eggs! We feel we have scored gold.

Our local grocery store reinstitutes its to-go service. We can hunt for food on its website with ease, we think. All the slots are full, but the website says to check back in early morning. We check at 7:15 but all the slots are full again. Next morning, the same. One morning I wake at 1:30 and check. All slots full. Our hope melts into a puddle. The stress threatens to fill every nook and cranny of our small house.

I figure out that the store's "check back in the early morning" means 12:00 a.m., so we wait up. Anxiously, iPad in hand, adrenaline pumping, we wait for the clock to strike midnight. Instantly I poke the "reserve a time" and frantically press the little circle next to a time, any time. The site crashes. We freak out. I keep pushing buttons. And...'submit your order' comes up on the screen. We did it, we did it! Laughter. High fives. Two minutes later, all of the slots are filled. I picture high fives in houses all over Cheshire County, and more than a few sad and discouraged.

We find out the next day that, unfortunately, this turns out to be an in-store pick up rather than curbside. We prepare to go into the fire and don our battle gear. Full respirator mask, rain poncho, sunglasses, gloves and hat. This time I'm only slightly embarrassed. The enemy is real. We gather our weapons. Hand sanitizer, disinfectant wipes, and disinfectant spray. More people in the store now wear masks, but we would still get a prize at the Covid-19 costume show.

The process afterwards at the car is complex: put groceries in the trunk, take off ponchos inside out, pop off hat, pull off gloves inside out, spray Lysol on legs and shoes, including bottoms, wipe hands, wipe door handles and steering wheel.

Driving home we feel as if we robbed a bank without getting caught.

Once home, we put on fresh gloves, step in a bleach bath and then put on fresh shoes, wipe down packages, and leave nonperishables in bags to remain untouched for a week. Then we wipe down everything we've touched – housekey, doorknobs, stair railings, table. Clothes go in the washing machine. We sing Happy Birthday twice to thoroughly wash our hands and arms.

And then we collapse. We've been on high alert for two hours. If, with all our precautions, we get this virus, everyone is doomed.

We talk about how we can hunt and gather in a different way. We had planned to reduce the size of our vegetable garden, but now we expand it, calling the addition our Corona Garden. We order seeds and start tomatoes and peppers indoors, something we haven't done in decades.

We find a curbside service with a greater ease of snagging a time slot. Although 45 minutes away, this is easy: pop the trunk, wave goodbye. When they don't have flour or toilet paper or yeast or garbanzo beans, we remind ourselves of shortages during WWII, or how Laura lived in Little House on the Prairie. We can do without.

We pick up pizza at a drive-through. I pop the trunk, and my husband, wearing a mask, walks to the window. He grabs the box with a wipe and tells the person to keep the change. Later we reheat the pizza in our oven. We almost feel normal.

Our hunter/gatherer skills are honed, and we discover another food source. Dandelion greens. Our field is covered with these nutritious nuggets, and they're delicious sautéed in olive oil with a little salt, pepper, and garlic. We gather them with delight, our field of dreams.

Finally, sixty-three days after my Last Supper, we are paused, no longer food obsessed.

Nothing is the same. Everything is the same. Everything has changed. Some things have changed. Nothing has changed. Everything. Something. Nothing.

Spring has still arrived—those undaunted tulips and daffodils, alliums, lilies, hyacinths, and chives are evidence--even as I wonder if Mother Earth is fighting back. Killing off millions to save herself. I can't begrudge her. I want to save myself, too.

How Do You Birthday During A Pandemic?

M.D. Flyn

I have a unique relationship with my fourth child. She is too much like me. Some would call her strong willed. Some would call her hard-headed. Most would call her prickly. But she hides a tender filling. She was the first of my children to cry for roadkill. She is the quickest to defend a friend on the playground. Either way, she is unfathomable. What Feralchild expected for her eighth birthday was another mystery.

I began my strategy well in advance, asking her what kinds of gifts she would like. Asking her if that snack she liked would be a good birthday treat. Dropping hints and sometimes begging. Feralchild is blunt. If she knew what she wanted she told me. But what she wanted was what she always had, most of which would not be possible in a lockdown situation.

No class party with cat cupcake toppers on strawberry cupcakes. No family party with the cousins. No going to the movies, or the bowling alley, or to get ice cream. How do you manage the expectations of a soon-to-be-8-year-old enigma? I did everything I could to control an unpredictable situation. And I also had one birthday surprise up my sleeve.

How do you manage mom's anxiety during a pandemic? I bought the gifts far in advance, in case of supply or shipping delays. I bought fixings for cake and pantry-friendly treats the month before. I timed the monthly shopping trip so we had her strawberries and watermelon in time for her birthday.

Then, the day after our shopping trip, she was talking to her older sister. We were sitting in the kitchen, Feralchild's feet swinging while she sat on a stool directly in front of Vic, demanding their full attention. She told her all about what she wanted, "strawberry everything, and cat everything. And ice cream cake." Vic saw my look of horror over Feralchild's head. We would have to go back out. My poor quarantine birthday girl could not go without ice cream cake.

We also faced the dilemma of delivering cat cupcake toppers. Every year Feralchild gives her classmates little cat figurines. This year she still wanted to give her friends their cats. I decided we would have to hand deliver them. How do you do that safely, while in quarantine? Ninja cat delivery. We drove around to each friend's house. Feralchild leapt out of the car, dashed to the mailbox, and hung the package off the mailbox at each house. Doing this safely was stressful for mom, but fun for Feralchild.

The night before her birthday, Feralchild was wired. She could not sleep. It didn't matter that she didn't get a party or get to see her friends or cousins. She was still dying for her birthday.

Finally, her birthday arrived. Feralchild demanded that we have cake and ice cream for lunch so she could open her gifts early. She got strawberry everything. There were strawberry marshmallows, strawberry jello with strawberry slices, and strawberry shortcake. Strawberry ice cream cake, kiwi strawberry juice, and strawberry lemonade. And giant strawberries tucked between each finger to make strawberry monster claws. Sticky sweet strawberry juice all over her face. And macaroni and cheese.

After we ate and tried to clean her face up, she opened her presents. It was a catstravaganza - she got a caticorn, some wild cat figurines, a cat sewing kit, and a cat wall decal. And a big bin of legos.

Her birthday surprise was still to come. It was the one thing I couldn't control and had to trust someone else to deliver. At the appointed time, I took the kids outside. We put lawn chairs out on the front lawn, six feet away from the street. You could smell that fresh, furiously growing air, like spring stretching her fingers out through the dirt. We waited, somewhat patiently. Feralchild less than others. Finally we heard a siren and saw a line of cars coming down the street. Our honorary grandma had arranged a birthday parade. They decorated the cars with signs, balloons, and ribbons. Friends and neighbors waved as they drove by. Some tossed small bags and cards for Feralchild. She happily waved, clutching her cat figurines in her sticky fingers as they passed. When

I watched the video later it only took a minute for them to pass, but it was one of the longest, happiest minutes of my life.

When I asked her later, Feralchild said her favorite part of her birthday was the parade. All my fretting over the food and the presents and the missing classmates didn't matter. She was just happy to see some of her friends. We connected without touching, six feet apart and waving.

photograph by the author

Grounded

Barbara Snow

"You're grounded," my dad said to me when I was fifteen. He had just found a pack of cigarettes in my coat pocket.

"You can't ground me," I said. "I'm a straight A student (true) and I was just keeping those for a friend (false)."

"Yeah, well now you're a straight A student who's grounded and you can tell me who the friend is so I can call their parents," was his response.

Fifty years later I can't remember if I served my whole grounded sentence, but I know my dad, who's been gone now for eighteen years, would not like being grounded during Covid-19. He was always going somewhere, doing something, meeting someone. "Like a fart on a griddle," Mom used to say, which has the distinction of being both crude and accurate at the same time.

Being grounded feels different now. A necessary pause in activities. An opportunity to see what happens when everything goes quiet for a while. A moment to look inward instead of always looking out. I find this both exhilarating and terrifying. What if I look inward and don't like what

I discover? I text my primary care physician and ask for a renewal of my Xanax prescription.

From my small apartment in south Minneapolis I have a stunning view of the city which outwardly does not look changed at all. But walking down the street towards it, I notice the lack of car and foot traffic and with so many jets grounded I see and hear birds – robins, jays, cardinals, sparrows, hawks, and the occasional eagle soaring overhead. I pass by my favorite local coffee shop – closed – and worry that the owner might never reopen. I wrote two plays in that coffee shop. It feels like my second home. The inner workings of my city have been altered significantly by this virus.

Things get grounded for a reason. Electrical appliances are grounded to allow excess electricity from a surge to flow outside of the home and back into the earth thus avoiding frying everything and everyone inside. Too much energy can be a bad thing for a refrigerator. Or a person. Or a planet.

Maybe Mother Earth just needed a break from us. It's not like she hasn't been sending out warning signals for oh, I don't know, the last fifty years, which we have done our damnedest to ignore. My dad used to say that everything in nature needs to be in balance or something bad will happen. Too many of any one animal and a disease occurs that kills as many as it takes to bring them back in balance. Let's face it, we have been out of balance for some time now. Between the climate change nay-sayers, capitalism at its very worst, and dare I add, Twitter, it feels like too much energy is going everywhere but back into the earth.

Being grounded felt very ungrounded during the first couple weeks of the mandated stay-at-home order. My routine vanished. No coffee at the art institute, no twice-weekly lecture classes on Asian art at the University of Minnesota, no volunteer activities at the Hennepin County History Museum. Breakfast, lunch, dinner with friends – gone. Worst of all, no travel plans to make. Since retiring eighteen months ago, travel has been my one luxury. Now my bucket list of places to go is limited to the grocery store, hardware store, or pharmacy. I think that's been a harder adjustment for me than eating my own barely adequate cooking.

About a month into the stay at home order I started waking up in a panic. A cough or a pain in my back or a headache - all convinced me I had IT. I resisted the urge to call my clinic because I knew this was my secret hypochondria kicking in bigtime. But it was paralyzing, this fear, so I decided that the only way to combat it was to develop a new routine. I pulled up an empty excel spreadsheet on my laptop and labeled four columns: Date, Time, Type of Activity, Completed. I entered activities in half hour increments from eight in the morning until six at night. It seems silly now: reading for one hour in the morning. Walking in the neighborhood for an hour in the morning and a half hour at night. Core exercises and stretching during the evening news. Spanish lessons in the morning on-line, Spanish grammar lessons by book in the afternoon. I put a check mark after each activity upon completion. I followed this schedule rigidly for about a month until I become grounded in this new routine. And the panic attacks subsided, at least for now.

My mom lives in a senior high rise that has been in lockdown for close to three months. I can no longer pick her up and take her on the little adventures she loves - like driving through Lakewood Cemetery to feed the big flock of wild turkeys cracked corn that I keep in the trunk of my car at her insistence. Now I can only see her through double glass doors when I drop off her groceries or prescriptions once a week. She waves at me through the doors, and I wave back at her before getting in my car and having a good cry. She looks smaller every time I see her. In her own implacable way, my mother has adapted to being grounded better than I ever will.

As I write this, it's spring in Minnesota. If there's one thing I'm grateful for in the midst of the pandemic, it's that we aren't starting the shutdown in November. The thought of spending the entire winter – again, this is Minnesota so we're talking about at least six months - cooped up in my apartment with no opportunity to venture out due to the snow and extreme cold would be intolerable. That is why I can't focus on the very real possibility of a second wave this fall. Not yet. Instead I'm going to stay focused on now. I'm going to make sure my excess energy isn't harming people, animals, and the earth. I'm going to keep looking inward to see what I have that may be useful to myself and others. I'm going to remember my dad's advice about finding the balance in nature. I'm going to keep waving at my mom through the double glass doors. I am grounded in my resolve to do this for as long as it takes.

The First Month in the Plague Year

William Bryk

A moose is haunting Antrim. It was seen near my house from a northbound car on Clinton Road last week. I know this because, as I was walking south, the passing car reversed, passed me, and stopped about 600 feet ahead. I waved to its driver as she resumed her trip north. She stopped. She was quite excited: she'd seen a moose in the woods. By the time I got to where she'd stopped, it'd moved on.

Its photograph made the front page of the *Stone Bridge Post*, a local weekly published from Hillsborough <http://stonebridgepostnh.rocks/wp-content/uploads/2020/04/Stone-Bridge-Post_2020_04_24-1.pdf>. The caption suggests that, unlike most of my neighbors, the animal has no plans to shelter in place.

I faintly recalled a rock-and-roll hit single with a Scottish flavor from 1958, released on Decca: "Hoots Mon," which has this lyric:

There's a moose loose aboot this hoose!

Though a cliché about Scots pronunciation, it's a reality in Antrim, New Hampshire.

Sheltering in place and social distancing against the corona virus is fairly easy in rural New

Hampshire. My house is a quarter-mile from the nearest neighbor and five miles from downtown Antrim.

By March 21, most institutions in Antrim and the surrounding Monadnock region had closed. Town Hall, the public library, the gym had closed. The Antrim branch of the Bank of New Hampshire transacted business only through its ATM and drive-in window. Even my riding lessons had been cancelled.

I'd been elected to the Antrim Planning Board on March 10, took the oath of office at Town Meeting on March 12, and was notified on Friday the 13th that no town boards would meet before May, if then. The job has no salary. Now it has no duties. Somehow that all balanced out.

So I stay safe, if only because there is little to do besides reading, writing, emailing friends to be sure they're well, tending to the cats, and walking.

I walk for an hour or more every day, south on Old North Branch Road to Clinton Road, past Old Pound Road to Miltimore Road to Smith Road and back. There is little automobile traffic.

I realized a pedestrian may notice many things that might be overlooked from a car.

Since the beginning of April, I've seen pairs of wild turkeys crossing the road. In warmer weather, flocks of them, young and old, pass through my property, pecking for seeds and insects. A doe and her fawn occasionally stroll through.

My cats recline on the deck and watch.

Along Clinton Road, Duke, a pit bull; a golden retriever; or a black Labrador often charge to the edges of their properties, barking fiercely to protect their people and their turf, tails wagging to show essential friendliness. I say hello and keep walking.

I noticed some trees posted with NO TRESPASSING signs. This seemed unfriendly and out of character for my neighbors. Then the *Monadnock Ledger-Transcript*, a bi-weekly published from Peterborough, published several items about an incident in Francestown, about 15 miles away. On Thursday, March 3, 2020, a resident discovered a deer stand on their property. It'd been placed there without the resident's knowledge.

A deer stand is a hunter's platform. It may lean against a tree, secured with cords or cables, or be freestanding, with three or four legs. Deer hunters have a better shot at their prey from a stand.

Apparently in response to an inquiry from the Francestown police, the New Hampshire Fish and Game Department opined that, as the resident's property was not posted, no crime had been committed by the unknown trespassers who had placed a structure on the resident's property without permission. Apparently hunters have the right to pursue their prey without regard for unposted property in New Hampshire. I thought of English foxhunters riding roughshod through a farmer's fields: "The unspeakable in pursuit of the uneatable," as Oscar Wilde wrote in *A Woman of No Importance.*

Of course, turkeys are very eatable. But once I learned New Hampshire's turkey season begins May 1, I bought four signs to post my property against hunting. I do not consent to hunters' entry upon my land to slaughter innocent creatures of God.

One of the landmarks along my walk is Old Pound Road. Quite sensibly, it's named for the Old Pound. Built in 1818, the remains of "this once critical municipal facility" stand at the southwest corner of Old Pound Road and North Holt Hill Road, about 1,000 feet from Clinton Road. Having detoured to see it, I know the Old Pound's ruins are about 28 feet square. Despite decades of "frost action and gravity," its stone walls still stand about four feet high and two feet thick.

In the 19th century, stray farm animals, when found and captured, were brought to the

Pound for safekeeping until the animals' owners came forward to collect them. Perhaps the townspeople were following these Old Testament commands (Deut.22, 1-2 (*King James Version*)):

> 1. Thou shalt not see thy brother's ox or his sheep go astray, and hide thyself from them; thou shalt in any case bring them in again unto thy brother.
>
> 2. And if thy brother be not nigh to thee, or if thou know him not, then thou shalt bring it into thine own house, and it shall be with thee until thy brother seek after it, and thou shalt restore it to him again.

The Old Pound was a matter of public safety. As local historian Charles Butterfield wrote, a stray animal could, "trample gardens, forage crops, break down fences, desecrate the cemetery, and foul or block the roadways...a free-roaming cow was no joke when people lived on what they grew and harvested."

The Pound Keeper's fees were 30 cents a day for feeding an animal and three cents a day for his trouble. The animal remained impounded until all fees were paid. If the owner disagreed with the fees, the town's board of selectmen chose an arbitrator to settle the matter. If no one came forward, the beast was sold, the keeper recovered his fees from the proceeds of sale, and the surplus was deposited in the town treasury.

The last known Pound Keeper, Mr. Morris Woods, held the title for decades. He was locally renowned for driving his Model T truck at little more than a walking pace. He took all morning to travel to and from downtown Antrim. Mr. Butterfield gently wondered whether Mr. Woods would have been fast enough to catch a pig.

***

The first creature I saw on my property after moving here in March 2016 was a beaver, slowly moving toward the wetlands, its tail occasionally flapping. Since then, ducks and other waterfowl cruise the pond during the summertime. Herons gracefully alight on the pond and as gracefully take flight, weaving between the trees.

Twice, stray hounds climbed to the door and persistently sought entry to the house. Wrestling with a very big, friendly, wriggly dog who wants to only come in so he can lick you to death is a challenge. Happily, a call to the Antrim Police Department brought the kindly and very strong Officer John Giffin to the door. He befriended each animal and persuaded it into his patrol car. The APD quickly found their owners, each of whom telephoned their thanks, one of whom brought jars of homemade jam.

Some bears passed by my pond in early April 2020. I know this because I found about a dozen piles of scat along the shore. They probably drank, relieved themselves, and moved on. This was over the weekend: on the following Monday, it snowed heavily, allowing me to put off picking up the scat for garden manure until the snow had melted. I used a manure rake and a bucket: learning to ride and to clean up after horses has taught me about shoveling... stuff.

But I digress.

Just south of Old North Branch Road's intersection with Clinton Road is Meetinghouse Hill Road, which the town abandoned over half a century ago. Although it appears on the town map, it's little more than a narrow depression between the trees. Apparently popular with the riders of All-Terrain Vehicles (ATV) and Off Highway Terrain Vehicles (OHTV), it's so deeply rutted that passage is nearly impossible even for a pedestrian.

I'd walked about a quarter-mile up the remains of Meetinghouse Hill Road before giving up and turning back. As I reached Clinton Road, I heard a raven's harsh croak and then saw him aloft, wings flapping to rise further into the sky. All this recalled a passage from C.J. Stone's *The Trials of Arthur*:

> *The raven is old, old. As old as time. As old as the mountains. As old as the trees. It has seen many things. It has observed the works of nature and of men. It has watched with an indifferent eye as dynasties have come and gone, as buildings were raised and then crumbled, as the works of men shone and then decayed. It has seen the motorways cutting swatches through the landscape like thin grey ribbons, and it has known that these things too would fall into disrepair and ruin. All things come from nature. All things return to nature. This the raven knows.*

Fashion Notes for the Well-Dressed in the Age of Corona

Larry Lefkowitz

With my slim mask and latex gloves, I feel like a surgeon and fear that in my walk from my house confinement to get some fresh air or food, I will be mistakenly pulled off the street and into a hospital to help out during the corona crisis. I prefer "Corona" to 'Covid-19. As the latter name hints that there were 18 previous plagues.

The gloves are hard for big-handed me to pull on without ripping them. The right-handed one proved a challenge when my shoe-lace untied during my walk and I had to retie it.

As for masks, there are a number of possibilities. I have mentioned the narrow one I use, "The Surgeon's Helper," I dubbed it. It is held by two strings tied to ears which, though not designed for this purpose, work quite well.

But there are more impressive masks. Such as the Black Bart triangular mask, made from a bandana, which is also helpful if you want to rob a bank. You protect your identity and, at the same time, protect the bank teller against your coughing corona virus on him.

There are also flowered masks (I group them under the name "Woodstock masks"). These are often self-made, or chosen, by the optimists and good souls among us.

After your outside stroll, you must of course remove, and dispose of your mask and gloves. Following which you should wash your hands thoroughly or poor alcohol on them. I prefer the former, although a drink of alcohol of the whisky type afterwards is also an anti-corona procedure (supporting one's mental state), especially if you are confined to remaining indoors (also known as quarantined).

In the coming days, more advanced means of protection against the virus will surely arise, such as modified astronaut's suits and mask, the suits hopefully will be available in pastel colors.

Tranquilizers: Drink a Corona Mexican beer and/or smoke a Corona cigar, applying the homeopathic medicine principle of "like cures like."

Deadlines to Lifelines

Jess Gerrior

COVID-19 has invited me back in to joys I have neglected for the business of "normal" life. Acorns for food. Collecting from under the oak at the front of my property with my daughters on a bright, cool day. Rinsing, shelling, sorting, rinsing, soaking, rinsing, soaking, rinsing, soaking, rinsing... anticipating the roasting, grinding, baking, tasting. Slowing. Savoring. Realizing. What we experience as unbelievably laborious, because we're accustomed to a world where food is provided in packages, branded and delivered to shelves, requiring no effort from us other than to drive our gasoline-powered vehicles to the store, in another life, would simply be normal, simply what we do, simply part of the flow. Appreciating our ancestors. Admiring the tenacity and enduring hope of oak trees.

photograph by the author

COVID-19 has alarmed me into redoubling my garden efforts. This is not a hobby anymore. This is vital. This is urgent. This is the truth that renders our previous, contrived systems practically obsolete. It wakes me into the reality that our calendars, a useful invention in a certain context, say, institutions of banking, the military, industry, education - are reasoned but ultimately futile attempts to predict and control time. Mother Nature, wisely, has never endorsed such idiocy. Farmers know this. Not only am I growing much more food, I'm growing it much more carefully; planning for succession and inter-cropping and stacked functions, and most of all, unpredictability. With the strain on global food systems and lack of local food security, COVID-19 hands me the impetus to do what I've wanted for so long - homestead - but could justify stalling until now. Deadlines are falling away, and replaced by lifelines.

photograph by the author

Couch Rash and COVID-19

Roxanne Rubell

Get up. Feed the birds. Feed the cats. Make coffee. Warm up water for a cup of lemon water. Drink cup of lemon water and gag a little because it's not always so easy going down first thing in the morning. Pour coffee into favorite mug. Add milk and stevia. Go yell at squirrels who are robbing the bird feeders – and birds of all their seed. Walk upstairs to office. Settle in. Read Wall Street Journal's The 10-Point: A Guide to the Day's Top News while simultaneously getting distracted by online sales at Kohl's or some other retailer. Check email. Contemplate the day. Lay towel across my thighs to protect them from Smokey's claws before he jumps up into my lap.

Except for talking to my cats, trying to chirp like a chickadee and yelling at the seed stealing, gluttonous, greedy squirrels, I've not spoken to a soul all morning. It is weird.

I suppose that those with significant others and families might envy my situation – alone with solitude at every turn. However, too much of a good thing is not good.

And why am I not making the most of a seemingly endless amount of free time? I know I should be creating something but...anxiety has me stuck, unable to start anything new. Anxiety is the angel in my house and as much as I want her gone, I just can't kill her – I don't have the energy right now.

On gray, rainy, glum days like today, I don't know what to do with myself. Sleep? Too much of a good thing on that front these days. After getting up around 7 AM, I find myself taking back my sheets around 10:30 AM and then waking up at 12:30 - just in time for lunch.

Eating. It's what I've been doing best right now. A gallon of salted caramel chocolate truffle frozen yogurt over the course of this past weekend. An entire four cheese frozen pizza. A bottle and a half of sauvignon blanc between yesterday and this evening.

Hiking – yes I need to go. I'm getting couch rash from sitting on my ass, watching far too much TV when I should be doing THIS RIGHT HERE. Or putting some paint on a canvas. Or reading, or...

I should be doing this, I should be doing that, I should be doing anything other than what I'm not doing.

Doing some shopping online and spending money – discretionary income that I should have more discretion about actually tapping into when I should be doing...something.

It's early afternoon and I still haven't spoken to a human.

Parents sequestered with kids at home are no doubt ready to pull their hair out or start day drinking to cope with the feeling of being trapped, smothered, unable to breathe due to restricted access to social oxygen from the outside. There's nowhere to go to, nowhere to run to these days. Perhaps a trip to the grocery store could be the ticket, where standing in line to even get into the store will swallow up 20 minutes of mindless time. That's 20 minutes less in what is already an agonizingly slow passage of time each day.

Maybe I should take a shower today.

And, I <u>should</u> do something productive.

Read more. Learn a new language using Babel. Take an Udemy online class and improve my Excel skills. I just don't feel like it. A zoom call with someone? Meh. I'd love to have someone to play Scrabble with but there's no one else here but me. Wait, not true, I <u>can</u> play Scrabble – there's an app!

If wringing my uninspired self's neck in hopes that <u>that</u> might somehow kick some measure of inspiration back into gear would work, I would do it.

What day of the week is it anyway?

It is sad to be wishing the days away like this. It is spring but all the hope and reawakening that should come with the season are heavily clouded, with a cloying uncertainty.

Purgatory on a daily basis. And as the daffodils bloom and the crocuses crown through the soil, we should be grateful. But a slow, dissolving vibrancy of spirit and not knowing the how deeply this virus will impact life as we know it, makes it hard to fully appreciate their seasonal splendor.

Where to go? Nowhere. What to do? Everything and nothing at all.

I know I'm not alone - we all feel powerless, as a state of limbo forcefully weaves itself into everyone's story.

I guess I'll go get the mail now.

Untitled

M. Allyson Szabo

When they shut down the whole of New Hampshire, I was taken aback. I mean, this thing was scary, and I didn't want to get it, but sending everyone home? When the lists came out, of who was essential and who wasn't, it didn't make any sense. Everything was so confusing. Every day I read about more people getting sick, and the effect the illness was having on them, and my anxiety spiked.

I'm a stay-at-home mom, and I'm an author, so working from my home in Jaffrey, NH, is normal for me. My sister is a teacher, and she was sent home to teach, so I gave up my office space to her. After all, I could use my laptop anywhere. Her husband already worked from home most of the time, so there wasn't a big change there. Then the grandson's daycare asked if his space could be given (free) to a first responder's kid, and we mulled it over and said yes.

The toilet paper shortages were interesting. We had just purchased a big pack before it happened, so we weren't in any kind of emergency situation, but it was still a bit unnerving. Yeast disappeared, too, but we buy a year's worth each

January, so I wasn't worried about that. The first time I went to Market Basket after the shut-down, and had to wait outside in line, it was intense. Going inside, wearing a big filter mask (because people in my home are immuno-compromised and I couldn't risk bringing anything back home), I felt very alone and small.

Most of my brands were gone, and I quickly realized that I needed to switch to emergency cooking methods, where you make what you have rather than planning meals and shopping for them. Once I changed headspaces, it went just fine. I picked up chicken and ground beef, the only real options at the time. I got canned ham, and tuna, and chicken, and some oysters as a treat. The big shocker was the price of eggs. Normally, in the spring, eggs are $1.29 for 18, and here I was paying $4.99 for 18. It hurt, but I dealt with it.

Our family has always worked to be prepared for emergencies. We had a couple of weeks-worth of food stashed away, in beans and legumes, pasta, rice, and canned meats and fish. I know how to make a dollar scream for mercy, how to grind that last two cents into bread and roses. I had prepared for the Apocalypse, but hadn't expected it to come with WiFi and electricity.

What I was wholly, utterly unprepared for was the abject loneliness I felt. After all, this was no change at all for me, other than having a three year old terror at my feet in the mornings. I still worked from home. I still did all the same things. I did not feel the same things, though, and it spiked my anxiety high. How could I be anxious or lonely in a house with three adults, two teenagers, and an occasional three year old? But I did feel anxious, and I did feel lonely.

I could handle the lack of toilet paper. Missing out on foods was no big deal. Looming meat shortages didn't make me the least bit nervous. But the change? It was subtle and it really hurt, inside, in ways I could not describe if I tried.

Then there was the guilt. After all, the people I loved were all working from home, very early on. We weren't in any great danger, and I was extremely careful at bi-weekly shopping trips to thoroughly decontaminate. I didn't have any nurses or doctors in my family. I didn't have any fire fighters or first responders, or even grocery clerks or pharmacy counter people. We were all safe. I felt enormous guilt over the idea that I was safe at home, and everyone else was out there, working, in danger.

What was this danger? At first, it was coughs and fever, and an inability to breathe. Having had pneumonia several times, it caused me some concern, but we were all relatively healthy. I didn't expect it to be all that bad. After a few weeks, we began to hear about blood clotting issues, though. Toes that turned odd colors. Lungs full of clotted tissue that no ventilator could fix, because they destroyed the parts that it would have helped. The silent menace of the unknowing carrier of disease, too, loomed over our quiet little home. Anyone could have this, and not know it.

We don't know how many people are actually dying of the Rona. That's what I call it, the Rona, because all the other names are either too clinical or too insulting. The Rona numbers are in the millions (3,693,452 cases, as of this writing), though not all of those are serious. But those millions don't actually mean anything. Not everyone who has it has been tested, because tests are still hard to come by. There are probably thousands, or hundreds of thousands, wandering around infected and not knowing.

The number of dead currently listed (255,551 people) probably isn't accurate either. We now know that there were people dying of the clotting part of the Rona, way back in February in California. How many died, and it was assumed to be a "simple" stroke or heart attack? In the beleaguered cities of New York City and Boston, in Italy and Spain and the United Kingdom, the dead are simply being tallied up, checked off as, "yes, this person had COVID-19 and therefore is a COVID-19 death" or "no, this person did not have COVID-19." We don't know if the Rona killed those people, though. No one's doing autopsies to see the real reasons, and honestly, cause of death is never a clean-cut thing, even in good times. These are not good times.

All of the uncertainty has opened my eyes to so many things. Everyone is stressed, and those of us who haven't had much change made to our lives are in some ways stressed out more than others. It's so hard to come to terms with the idea that you were already living in a sort of lock-down, when things were normal. It's even more difficult to understand how much different it is when it's necessary, and enforced. I would not have gone out last night, if things in New Hampshire were normal. But I wanted to go out last night, because I couldn't. I suppose we always want what we don't have.

FaceBook is a cesspool. Petty tyrants have taken to adjudicating over kangaroo courts, deciding who is guilty of whatever the crime de jour is. People who would normally be calm and thoughtful have become nasty, angry, and sometimes inappropriate. Nothing is the same; everything is different.

I try to remind myself it could be worse. We could be stuck indoors all the time, instead of out gardening in the backyard. We could be without the internet, which allows us to stay connected with friends far and near. We could have had family members furloughed, no longer being paid, trying to figure out how to pay the bills during this extended stay-at-home order, but we're not. We could have been completely unprepared, but we weren't. We were, and are, lucky.

Often, the reminding doesn't help. I find myself thinking the same terrifying thoughts, over and over again. What if someone I love gets this? What if I get this? What if someone dies? What if it's my best friend? What if it's one of the kids? What if? What if? What if?

And then my faith in humanity is restored. The local restaurant, Sunflowers, started making bulk items available to those of us who wanted them, and so I have big bags of flour and sugar and rice, to tide us over. Friends come by and "ding dong ditch" packets of seeds on my porch, tiny promises of hope, to be planted in my garden. The weather warms up, and I can feel the sun on my skin again. I play dress-up with my grandson, and we run around the yard in medieval clothing, planting seeds.

Every night, at 6'o'clock sharp, the bells ring. At first, it was just the churches in town, and me. Then others joined in. Now, each night there's a cacophony of bells ringing through the town, telling us we're not alone. We ring for first responders and helpers, for doctors and nurses and essential workers. I think, too, we ring for ourselves. Making noise is a proclamation that we're alive, that we're here, that we haven't given in to despair or fear.

And so I go on. My family goes on. I try to write each day, sometimes succeeding and sometimes failing. I edit when I can pull my brain into the game enough to do so. I make videos for YouTube, encouraging fellow authors and artists, and reenactors who are without fairs this year. I do what I can to help others, and in doing so, I help myself. I guess that's what it's all about!

Circle Up

Jennifer Tirrell

It was abdominal exercise day. On my back on the living room floor I finished counting to 30 and panting, out of breath, I laid still for a moment, my eyes seeing nothing but the white of the ceiling above me. I started thinking about Laura, the 31 year old niece of a dear friend who was fighting for her life at Mass General Hospital. Immediately, I lifted her up in prayer, as I was in the habit of doing whenever she came to mind, as well as during my scheduled prayer times. After I finished, I opened my eyes and the underside of a violet plant that I had received caught my attention. From my unusual vantage point, I saw for the first time that purple veins ran through the whitish green on the bottom of the leaves. The veins presented as a swollen tangle of beauty, and my gaze sat on them for some time before I went back to my exercises. I tried to remember what the other side of the leaves looked like and it seemed to me they were emerald green and maybe even fuzzy.

Afterward, I was sitting on the couch. It was the 8th week of the Covid-19 quarantine and boredom felt quite natural. In a semi-daze, wondering what I could busy myself with next, the violet once again caught my attention. This time, I was seeing the top of the plant and I noticed the leaves were, indeed, a luscious shade of dark green with just the tiniest bit of fuzz covering their verdure.

Two days later, I was again on my back, completing my second abdominal workout of the week. I smiled a hello at the veiny undercarriage of the plant. Because of the big Q, I found myself making friends with many living things that I previously had overlooked. The weeks of solitude at home had me in a state of mindfulness like nothing I had experienced in the past. It was as though my life was now one long meditation--whether in prayer, at the window, or while taking a solitary walk. I noticed that the stems of the plant had tightened together and were reaching upward more than they had been two days before. While on the couch in my usual afternoon position, I observed that a tiny stem had appeared in the middle of said leaves, which were now extra puffy, like a pillow that had been plumped up, ready for company. I imagined them gathering around the little stem, cheering as it sprouted and began to grow. The next day, there was another little stem, and two days later, a third and fourth.

By Sunday, the first stem was budding, showing a faint purple visible only to those who had eyes to see it. (In this case, there was only me, for my daughter, home from NYC for safety reasons, spent her days sequestered in her room, working at her desk near the window.) Crossing to the sink, I opened the faucet and poured my violet friend a drink, my way of adding encouragement to this gift of blossoming that was sure to arrive any day now.

While gently pouring out the life-giving water, my thoughts again turned to Laura. Just then, my phone pinged. It was my friend reporting on her niece. Laura had been unconscious for 40 days. The number 40 signifies a long time and has biblical significance; 40 days in the wilderness, 40 days and 40 nights of flood, 40 days in the desert. She went on to say she looked forward to what God had in store for Laura next. Surely, healing was imminent. After I read the text, I stared at the weak little stem and closed bud that was seemingly held up by the strong leaves tightening ranks around it. I thought of Laura as the tiny stem, and all the people around the world that were praying for her as the leaves.

By Wednesday the flower had blossomed. The two top petals were a rich purple-violet, while the 3 lower petals were a lovely mix; dark on the edges and fading to the lightest possible shade closest to the yellow stamens. The other stems had buds that were slowly rising up from underneath the blooming flower. In the midst of thanking God for the beauty of the small violet, I did not find it surprising when an update on Laura arrived with a ping.

"Laura's doing amazing and is more "awake" the text read. "She responded to the nurse talking to her and even squeezed her right hand on command." The text went on to say that the nurse FaceTimed with Laura's sister so Laura could hear and then asked Laura to open her eyes. I blinked away tears of joy and thankfulness as I read further. "She opened them SUPER wide for us. She is gonna come back to us. She's already starting!!!!"

Nature reveals to us, when we take a long and thoughtful look, what our eyes might not see otherwise. Changing my perspective allowed me to notice small changes, and alerted me to bigger possibilities. Likewise, although we are separated in many ways by the Covid-19 virus, we can intensify our focus toward one another from afar—circling around in love and uniting in prayer. And when we do, we better get ready. God's not going to run out of miracles anytime soon.

Pandemic Notes: The Forty-Fourth Day

Maura MacNeil

"It is better to live in a state of impermanence than in one of finality" Gaston Bachelard

ꕥꕥꕥ

On the forty-fourth day of the pandemic, my sister, ten month's dead, begins to visit me.

ꕥꕥꕥ

In a link to an article a friend emails to me, I read about the strange and vivid dreams so many people are experiencing since we began to shelter in our homes; increased anxiety and decreased sleep heightens REM, leading to this new intensity of dream.

ꕥꕥꕥ

Since the second week of March I have been hypervigilant with worry. I worry about viral aerosols of COVID-19 lurking everywhere I go. When in public my ear is tuned for the coughs of others. I worry about having enough paper masks until the sturdier cloth one I buy online arrives, whether I have enough hand sanitizer, toilet paper. I worry whether my immune system is strong enough to withstand the virus if I contract it from germs left behind by the delivery driver on an Amazon package. Is my husband washing his hands enough? Are his lungs strong?

ஒ ஒ ஒ

I want to believe that the dreams of my sister are something other than the product of anxiety. I want to believe she is, in fact, coming to check on me, to watch over me. Over a period of two weeks she returns over and over in dream, almost every night, and each time I wake to the dark quiet of the house and am filled with a longing and grief that feels like large stones weighted on my chest that leave me breathless.

ஒ ஒ ஒ

If my sister were alive I would add her to my worry list. There would be daily phone calls filled with musings on the way that life feels so uncertain, so tenuous. We'd find humor at the absurdity of hoarding toilet paper. I would tell her that for the first time in my life I have counted the number of rolls in my house. We would commiserate about shared concerns for her health as she had no choice but continue dialysis three days a week at the clinic in order to stay alive.

ൿൿൿ

My dreams contain my sister and me at various ages in homes we have lived within. We are teenagers putting on makeup in front of the bathroom mirror; we are young children playing dress-up with our mother's clothes in the large closet of a shared room; she is newly married and cooking in my grandmother's kitchen. She speaks to me from across the living room in our family summer home, and when I wake I can't remember the conversation, but the distinct cadence of her voice follows me for the rest of the day.

ൿൿൿ

Daily I move back and forth through the borderland of what was once and what is now, a muddy soup of containment and worry, grief and silence. My sister arrives in a shadowland, the verge of something wild and astonishing and dark with occasional cracks of light that rise to the surface of the boiling soup that the virus has demanded we eat.

❧❧❧

Just as she suddenly appeared, she suddenly disappeared. She was with me and then she was gone. I grieve the loss of her in my dreams in the way I grieve the loss of my childhood home or the life that once was that will not reappear again. My attention now drawn to the immediate: death tolls and the collision with memory. The way *what once was* is a reminder of impermanence. I am waking before daylight and enter mornings with the spring abundance of wren and finch and sparrow territorial song, the scent of lilac blooms unfurling that provides reverie of a past. This, too, will pass as summer deepens.

Untitled

Ann Day

Looking back over my life of ninety years I don't remember being lonely or bored. There never seemed to be enough hours in the day. Even if I am with people, part of me wants to be outside exploring, climbing, running, following a new path in the woods, taking notes and photos to write about.

I have written poems, essays and stories in many genres. I am still writing a nature column for a local paper after nearly fifty years and taken many photos to try to illustrate my desire to communicate with our Natural world from cockroaches in Nicaragua to a cow moose in the woods of Vermont.

From growing up in a family of five girls (I am the oldest) to boarding schools and camps and operating a guest farm, I was with people almost all the time. Even with two roommates and communal dining, I still found ways to be by myself in the woods, a mossy nook where I could be one with the trees and plants and wildlife. I have always liked writing and sharing my love of nature and adventure with others that way.

The Pandemic and resulting lockdown here at Rivermead has not really drastically changed my routine. In some ways it is even easier to keep to a certain schedule. However, I find myself confused and preoccupied more than usual. Perhaps it is because I will be 91 on July 1st. Perhaps it is because I do not have the stimulus of the personal contacts with people.

I feel blessed I can still walk to the woods and trails. I can watch and listen to a variety of species of birds and plants that grow here. Always exciting discoveries as I become one with trees, wetlands and the river.

This is not changed because of the coronavirus. It actually has added to the depth of my learning. And to the sadness I feel every day. I have become even more grateful for being able to be part of this natural world.

I am
the meadow, the mud,
the early blossoms
of red osier, the cattails,
the red-winged blackbird,
the breeze that bends
willowed grasses
and emerging spring
that buds within me.

Difference Between Alone and Lonely

Pamela Erdmann

"This (loneliness) is a cold bath. This removes almost all the advantages of living alone and amplifies all the hard parts." Coontz

Being alone in my elderhood has been like moving to a new country, new language, new customs, new rules where I can, for the first time in my life, be solely self-determined... No one tells me what to do and when to do it. I even have my first all-alone dog. The others, over the years, have had shared ownership and loyalties.

Having had four children by the time I was twenty-seven, I never had much alone time. In the beginning of aloneness, divorce, hurt, anger, pain, it wasn't a fun place to be. Remember walking down a street in Keene and seeing a middle aged couple and truly aching for that. A few years later, seeing the same, such a feeling of lightness and freedom. A little yearning to be sure but how the balance had shifted.

Alone, over these past thirty years, has meant adventures, travel: Wales, Finland, Ireland, Scotland, China, the Arctic; work in the prisons; taking in-person and on-line courses; and, most life changing, learning about, teaching, and studying

Mindfulness. No need to negotiate, just saying "yes!" to whatever caught my fancy and so much did.

I was also blessedly partnered for a good deal of that time with a gentle, loving, supportive older man, The strongest he would say about an adventure that didn't turn out so well was "Well, let's not do that again..." Sadly, he died ten-plus years ago and once again, alone.

Solitary, alone, choosing again freedom and adventure, always puzzled when folks ask me "How can you travel alone?" If I don't travel alone, no travel, no adventure. I chose how and where to live, why not where to go?

I also get to choose how and where I'll live. Downside is that there's no one to help with the chores so if I can't afford to hire, it just doesn't happen. No one ever died of a shaggy lawn or dump runs only once a week, or dust under furniture too heavy to move. I make the trade-off with pleasure.

Loneliness, I discovered, in this unimaginable pandemic, is a totally different village. It is dark, constricting, often terrifying. In this strange village lives a hoard of big and little creatures, dark, scraggly creatures who, I thought, had long been gone. Character "flaws," "unreasonable wants," constant judgments of self and others walk the streets regularly, sometimes even having parades dressed in a variety of disguises. I thought with all this Mindfulness and therapy they'd have been swept across the Atlantic, deep into the wide Sargasso Sea. Mostly they are from the Not Enough Clan, not enough smarts, money, kindness, skills, whatever, there's always something. Sometimes, they march with another family, the More Than Enough family forming a formidable battalion. It always puzzles me how easy they are to recruit. The More Than Enoughs also leave trails of guilt. "You're so... You could have done so much with that. Why didn't you?"

At eighty three, I'm growing very tired of this village and wish to move on to the Just Enough Village with its charming streets of Ease, Wonderment, and Contentment, all spilling off the wide main thoroughfare named In the Moment Boulevard. When I get here, it is spacious, quiet and roomy. Creativity springs from the bushes, wagging its tail like a happy pup. "Play with me! You look like fun!" none of the shame and heaviness that that other village houses.

Like every journey, one first has to decide where you want to go and why. Sometime you do research, sometimes it just pops up, here's where I go next. I didn't do my research on alone/lonely. As with other trips, when I don't do a minimum of research, I find surprises, both good and not so good. Aloneness had mostly good ones while loneliness... not so much. I miss hugs, eye contact, shared giggles, different opinions, even some of the squabbles.

Loneliness seems to collude with aloneness in removing any excuses for not sitting down and doing the writing I've talked about for years. Just do it, damn it! What else are you going to do? Another lesson from the pandemic, the more you put things off, the more they're in your face. And so here I am... at least it's a start.... And here's an ending found in an old journal.

"In all the years of taking drugs, being a therapist, having a guru, sufi dancing, whatever, I haven't gotten rid of one neurosis yet. The only difference is that instead of these monsters, there are these little schmoos now, and I just invite them in to tea."

Ram Das

Hats off to many more tea parties!

Poetry

We pause

Mary Sheehan

as the planet holds its breath.

Confusion envelops us
while the illness stomps its way through our walls
to ravish the weak and the sick

We throw the innocents to the front,
unprotected,
a medical Gallipoli.

As we hunker in our homes and hovels
the knowledge that we are better than this
bubbles down deep
where the phosphorescence dwells,
preparing to move.

Stages of the Virus

Amanda Burns

First we marveled at the virus
How it shuttered the largest school
Sent us home from our jobs
Gave us time with our families again

Then we cried at the pressure
Where's the money coming from?
Keeping the kids busy comes at cost
We are bored too...breaking

Our moods became pendulums
The grandfather clock swinging from
Joyful moments to utter despair
Economic and political fractioning

Then we grieved. God, we grieved
Over the dead and dying we know
And those we don't. We mourned
Our old life and the lost future

We keep waiting...we wait

Early Spring

Patricia Zube

The time to transplant trees is early spring
Before their roots awake from winter's rest
And buds swell plump to sun's warm beckoning.

Hard work awaits the elder man. He'll sing
Of younger days of supple strength his quest.
The time to transplant trees is early spring.

With spade in hand, where rocks and roots are
king,
He toils and tires and strains to do his best.
Will buds swell plump to sun's warm beckoning?

His autumn age reminds him with a sting
Physique and youth are lost, he must attest.
The time to transplant trees is early spring.

He pauses, wonders what the weeks will bring
To aching limbs. Will sleeping roots be blessed
And buds swell plump to sun's warm beckoning?

Oh, Nature, you're a cruel and joyous thing.
You wake his dreams of springtime splendor-
dressed.
The time to transplant trees is early spring.
And buds swell plump to sun's warm beckoning.

Untitled

Patricia Zube

bright daffodils bloom
perking up aching spirits
harbingers of spring
look to nature for relief
green trees are lungs of the world

A Lady with No Mask

Chen Yihai, author and translator
　　Rodger Martin, ed.
(In the time of Covid 19, March, 2020)

All day I wander my empty campus,
No one, no one, no one there until
I come across a lady.
But she wears no mask! She wears no mask.
She wears no mask because she is sculpture.

Beside the water she bows her violin,
Smoothly bows her violin, sweetly bows her violin.
What melody does she play? What melody?
The birds sang; they warbled,
They tremuloed, they trilled.

Strauss! "Spring Waltz." I waltzed. *I waltzed.*

Alone, she played alone, but an empty campus,
and all the singers listened to her play.

Chinese version of *A Lady with No Mask*

不戴口罩的少女

昨天去学校值班
没有遇见谁
只遇见了一个少女
她居然没有戴口罩
因为她是一个雕塑

她在水边拉着小提琴
一遍又一遍
她究竟演奏的是什么曲子呢

看到枝头叽叽喳喳跳跃的小鸟
我才知道
她演奏的是《春天圆舞曲》

她独自演奏
一座空荡荡校园和很多小鸟
在倾听

2020 年3月

The Stairs

Cai Ying Ming

On my days in captivity,
I grope from one word to the steps of despair, ask for patience.
Waiting for the moon to give the cold,
The wind and the pigeons blew through the iron window.
The long days are like every brick of this house
Until I also become a brick, lose the temperature
Piled up in the dim light.
People's best wishes are like birds perched on the treetops,
Will a cruise ship meet a sail?
Every window of the ship sparkles,
As if god had just wiped it with a rag.
Tourists return from the corners of the world,
The picture frame at home awaits you.
Will your heads be silenced like the lonely lamp of the sea?
And me, in the house in the countryside,
My meditation is like the ocean far away.
Have you touched the stairs of my language?
Please climb along the steps,
Please put on your life jackets tightly.
Climb the mountain of hope,
The sun shines and the epidemic vanishes like ice.
Life like a pure lily, blooms over the mountain.
Breathe freely as the sea's sound rushes into house and lungs.
The dusty window finally opens and I am revived in language.

Chinese version of *The Stairs*

梯子

在我禁闭的日子
我从一个词摸索到绝望的台阶，索求耐心
等待月光给予的冰凉
风与鸽子吹过铁窗
岁月蓝色得令人窒息
漫长的日子宛若这间房屋的每块砖块
直到我也成为一块砖，丧失温度
堆砌在昏暗的光线里
人们美好的愿望像小鸟儿停在树梢上
来年春天的相见
一艘游轮还能遇见一只船帆么
游轮的每间窗户闪闪发光
如同上帝用抹布刚刚擦过
从钻石公主号返回世界各地的游客
家里的相框等候你们
你们的头像会如大海的孤灯变得沉寂么
而我，在乡村的屋子
我的冥想一如那片遥远的海洋
你们抚摸到我语言的楼梯了么
沿着台阶爬上来吧

请紧紧套上救生服

攀登希望的山顶

太阳光耀大地，疫情如冰块消逝

生命如同纯洁的百合花，漫山遍野地开放

呼吸自由如海水涌进房子与肺部

尘封的窗终于敲开，我在语言中复苏

蔡英明

Sunset over Putnam's Field

Stephen Seraichick

The sinking sun cast yellow light
Like butter spread on the grass
And distant maples
Another day looking out
At my tiny verdant world
Happy that I made it this far
And coming to terms with what I missed
The journey of the sun
And the closing of the day
That marks our lives
We miss it most of the time
Too busy in our haste
Then a virus slows us down
To a crawl
And we're finally available
To "see"
And to wonder

Further Down the Road

Stephen Seraichick

Each of us has a story now;
One or two of which we'll tell over and over
Thirty years down the road.
The grandkids will want to hear them again and again
As their Moms and Dads leave the room.
Pain has a way of weaving a fabric of our most difficult memories
Like when you were young and someone your age
You knew well, passed away suddenly,
"How can that be?"
Suffering somehow substantiates our lives
Knowing the end is but one step away
Giving profound meaning to the last step we took.
What's the story you're weaving right now?
The one you'll tell down your own road years from now?
The one you'll tell over and over
Ad nauseum.
They'll be two high points:
One gut-wrenching humor
The other gut-wrenching sadness.

What the Hell is Normal?

Stephen Seraichick

There's nothing like a cold beer
During a pandemic
To take you out of your funk
Even if Jack, your next-door neighbor, has to stand six feet away
And pull off his mask off to tip one with you.
But it gets you thinking
What is normal anyhow?
And what was the normal we now so readily fawn over
Like a dreamscape that evaporated in the snap of our collective fingers?
Was it the way we did the same thing over and over again?
Or is it there never was a thing called normal
And that that bygone squeaky "normal" brought its own troubles to our doorsteps?

Is it perhaps, that change always changes
And that of all the species on this planet we are the masters of handling that?
Even though at times it really sucks!
"Oh, I have to adapt, damn!"
There are worse things like, for example,
Extinction.
I worked for a while in construction
And one of our crew was going to ask the love of his life for her hand in marriage
I'll always remember his words, "A man's gotta do what a man's gotta do!"
Normal is kind of like that.

Quarantine Song

Claire Golding

These are the comforts
sun and skin
bed and blanket
and the bones melt in
no hard world
just this room
chickadee, lilac tree
far from doom

These are the dangers
spit and spray
molecule, ridicule
cant, delay
no safe place
just one world
longitude, latitude
frayed and curled

These are the watchwords
PPE
separate, ventilate
EMT
too few masks
nonstop surge
isolate, intubate
face shield, dirge

These are the casualties
old and young
carnival, funeral
heart and lung
glad embrace
one last word
celebrate, graduate
vows all heard

These are the certainties
day and doubt
speculate, obfuscate
blame, cry, shout
grass turns green
bugs still bite
masticate, copulate
then comes night

These are the comforts
wine and tea
telephone, saxophone
us, them, we
trees in leaf
sky in blue
buttered bread, warmth ahead
we, us, you

The Lost Hour

Pravat Padhy

The old woman misses
The narration of the fairy tales
While lulling the children to sleep.

She is unable to rejoice:
Their tender smiles
Playing hide and seek
Moving her around
With a list of demands
Asking for chocolates
Helping for the homework:
Filling the gaps
And the spell checks.

The solitude
Like thick clouds
darkens her eyes.
She looks at herself
So different today
Lying on the quarantine bed.

The Dark Day

Pravat Padhy

He is driven to the isolation ward
He contours yesterday's rainbow of life:
Twin kids and his better-half
Strolling in the park
Swinging them in seesaw
Running after the butterflies
And searching the ball in bushes.

He dwells in the past
As if the clock stops for a while
Freedom of natural breath
Becomes a dream;
The sun stops shining.
Singing birds cease murmuring.

Somewhere the moon hides
Behind the fearful clouds
The twinkling stars
Perhaps he would never glance again
The distance between the beds:
The sun sets for someone
Another awaits
To enter into another darkness

Still, he dreams the world
Is alive outside
One day he will walk again
And greet his family in the
Fresh morning sunshine.

killer

M.S. Munro

i sit inside my four walls
waiting for it to strike
it hasn't come inside yet
but it is all around
a dark evil cloud of sick despair

my loved ones and friends
are safe... so far
but daughter, cousins, friends
fight on the front line
without gear or equipment
they race to face the
Enemy
to stop it.... to kill it

yet here i sit waiting...
waiting... waiting
and all i can do is pray

will it attack...will it die
what will happen?
all the world is changed
i cry but no one hears
i see the Mountain but
it does not speak to me

staring out the window...
slender golden sunlight
robins arrive
songbirds sing and trees
near bursting with buds
sway in the wind
they whisper
have hope my child
the light is coming

Into the Light?

Bill Chatfield

Everywhere across this nation
There's a COVID conversation
Not in coffee shops or stores
We don't go in there anymore.

Most talk is within four walls
With conversation at a crawl
But some is in the street
Protests with guns, signs, and feet.

We've lost track of what is normal
Our reactions sharply informal
In the darkness of perpetual night
Will we ever find the light?

Hancock Hideout

Julie A. Dickson

She's alone in her house,
her sanctuary in the woods
virus or not, lives ensconced
at the end of a long dirt drive,
animals her only companions.
Well-laid in larder, taught well
by a mother raised in the great depression,
she can survive for months
on fruits and vegetables canned
during long autumn days, while watching
gold and vermillion leaves flutter
past peach and apple trees
settling on the ground , a patchwork
quilt covering her many gardens,
seen from kitchen window.
Vivaldi or Bach on the stereo,
played 24 hours a day, background
sounds as soothing as the brook
flowing near her back yard,
sounds as benign as a yearling doe
wandering quietly the dense thicket,
or frolicking squirrels chasing around
fruit trees, flashes of red – cardinal
plucking a seed or nuthatch patiently
walking upside down on nearby tree.
They know nothing of a human virus,
neither does she, lone isolated woman
by choice, she lives solitary in her
hideout, surrounded by books,
rescued cat curled on her lap,
dog napping at her feet; she lives her life
as she has chosen – pandemic aside.

Wanton Weather

William Doreski

Snowfall wears a surgical mask
in this age of feckless disease.

Because it clings to every surface,
it risks spreading a virus

powerful enough to French-kiss
every virgin into a frenzy.

I'm afraid to go out and shovel
the spongy mess from the driveway.

Already I can taste its lewd
and acidic texture laving

over my face as I strain to lift
shovelful after shovelful

to only the faintest applause.
Let's stay indoors and watch it melt.

But you with your germproof snowsuit
have already rushed into the storm.

Before I get my boots laced up
you've cleared a path to the road

so the Mask of Red Death can find us,
if he happens to be on the prowl.

The daylight's too thick to swallow
without difficulty. The roar

of oil burner in the basement
reassures with the ancient language

of fire brought smartly up to date.
What would Faustus say if faced

with this slur of wanton weather?
Would he feel his soul collect itself,

don a parka, and set out to meet
the devil at the bend in the road?

I feel nothing but the snowfall
plastering every detail

to render the landscape rococo
and mock our aesthetic mood.

Ringing Difficult Changes

William Doreski

Do you hear a constant tingling
in your mind? Metal on metal,
it seeps from the recycling center
and lodges in the human genome,
where every hint is fodder.

The village clenches in misery
as, one by one, shops close forever,
unlocked doors banging in the wind,
unsellable goods abandoned,
tainted by criminal proteins.

We should stay home with doors
and windows sealed against smells
discolored by strong ultraviolet.
We should read those dreary books
we've been putting off for decades.

I think someone in a monk's robe
is ringing difficult changes
with a fervor dredged from the past.
Don't listen, don't try to understand—
the old bronze speaks in tongues.

We can't waste any more time
in our favorite café because
it went out of business, leaving
scorch marks on an old pine floor.
We can't expect the post office

to deliver us from evil.
The hardware store, source of many
unkempt noises, still accepts cash
or check, the elderly clerks
grinning like Jolly Roger.

Ignore any sound that suggests
we've passed into a digital gloom.
A lone crocus erupts in the yard.
Consider it the equivalent
of the last impromptu kiss.

Specialty Selections

William Doreski

Pushing her shopping cart past
stainless but vacant shelving,
the woman curses the hoarders
who in a time of pandemic
have seized the most usable goods.
But this is "Specialty Selections,"
a category alien to me
since I lack gourmet finesse.

She's from that other world—
professional, well-traveled,
literate without much reading,
but certain of what she's read.
Yet in her wool cap and hooded
winter coat, each an exact
shade of black, she looks angry
as the tubular men who stash

assault rifles and ammo where
the Feds will never find them.
"Choose organic—choose peace
of mind," reads a sign above
the long slats of useless display.
I wouldn't pay extra to preserve
my carcass beyond its sell-by date,
but she would have loaded her cart.

That long white wire running
from her pocket to her ear—
is she listening to Paul Simon
or Beyoncé or Bessie Smith?

She’s old enough to remember
Frank Sinatra in his prime,
but looks as if she’d disapprove
of his Jersey mob connections.

Unwilling to cocoon myself,
I don’t travel with digital tunes.
but prefer to hum inside my head,
devising little song-bubbles.
They burst and smear the surfaces
I’m afraid to touch with my hands

39 - Ringing Difficult Changes

Do you hear a constant tingling
in your mind? Metal on metal,
it seeps from the recycling center
and lodges in the human genome,
where every hint is fodder.

The village clenches in misery
as, one by one, shops close forever,
unlocked doors banging in the wind,
unsellable goods abandoned,
tainted by criminal proteins.

We should stay home with doors
and windows sealed against smells
discolored by strong ultraviolet.
We should read those dreary books
we’ve been putting off for decades.

I think someone in a monk’s robe
is ringing difficult changes
with a fervor dredged from the past.
Don’t listen, don’t try to understand—

the old bronze speaks in tongues.

We can't waste any more time
in our favorite café because
it went out of business, leaving
scorch marks on an old pine floor.
We can't expect the post office

to deliver us from evil.
The hardware store, source of many
unkempt noises, still accepts cash
or check, the elderly clerks
grinning like Jolly Roger.

Ignore any sound that suggests
we've passed into a digital gloom.
A lone crocus erupts in the yard.
Consider it the equivalent
of the last impromptu kiss.

The Crow

Elaine Reardon

A crow calls after I've poured
a second cup of coffee The forest is quiet,
aside from Moss Brook, splashing
sounds through an open window.

This morning one deer paused to browse
by the window. Woodfrogs which left
their clutch of eggs in the pond,
now have gone to quiet again.

That crow was only bird cawing this morning.
No birds answered as it flew, calling.
Have corvids socially isolated, too?
Yesterday I followed tracks

that came out of the forest
circled round the house,
hunted some small animal
that escaped up a white pine.

Spring is quieter this early May
aside from those wood frogs
who know how to have a good time.
Right at cocktail hour.

I almost hear Billy Strayhorn at
the piano, and see trays with appetizers
and drinks passed around the small
vernal pool, where passion runs

fast and loose, just past the garden.

Cannonau: A Glass of Wine

Rodger Martin

The Grenache—before Caesar, before Etruscans—
Sardinian vineyards; it's as earth and drink are one:
The Joshua Tree, history's Sequoia. Life's a spectrum.
Blood's three-dimensional, more than a pixilated screen.
Light is the lion come down to drink: Pride of the pride
Regis Rex in his ruddiness, his earthiness, his hide,
but here with this glass, between the poles of pixilation
and abstract depth, reside the larynx and its vibration,
the nasal take of oxygen, and the shaped tongue,
a choral embrace of that first Nuraghe song.

Cannonau: (KAN-non-NOW) A wine region of Sardinia
Light is the lion come down to drink from "A Glass of Water" by Wallace Stevens,
Nuraghe (nur-RAH-gey) The first people of Sardinia

Living with a pandemic

Denise Linnay

Today's different.
Tomorrow's uncertain.
Let's make the best of right now.

Vacation dreams?
Vaporized.
Home is life, work, and play.

Need a haircut?
Not a problem. Will it be
Ponytail, bowl cut, braid, dreadlocks, or shaved?

What shall I wear?
Wardrobe's brimming with choice.
Let's stay in pajamas, okay?

Feel like a snack?
Only one apple left.
But we've plenty of oatmeal, I see.

This pandemic is a strain on my nerves.
Isn't it strange
How little I need?

Living the Pandemic Nightmare

Denise Linnay

Terror creeps
outside my walls where
I remain
a prisoner by choice.

Its strident voice
beats fresh alarms
that fail to calm
my frozen heart.

I whimper, mew,
eyes squeezed,
ears keened to hear yet more.

The outside dread of
Others.

It
stretches far in wild kaleidoscopic color.

I chew my nails.
I gnaw raw knuckles.
I wince.
I pace.

There's no escape
the scrape of reaper's scythe
beyond my door.
And hence I hide.

I fear my madness -
a mad dash out,
to have it done and over with.

I cringe,
reduced to pallid shades of mediocre gray.

Exposed.
Undone.

Final wishes

Denise Linnay

It's an odd sensation this morning
Will this be my last day of good health?
The seventy-one-year-old man begging his doctor
to die with a view of the sky
This image most potent awakened a yearning
to meet my own death with a vision
of facing the forest, warmed by the sunshine, sung to by
Nature's own best

I want to feel breezes brush over bare arms
I want to see clouds drifting by
I want to hear raindrops kerplunking my body
I want to taste roses nearby
I want coolness to wash over my fingers
I want to meet death with a smile

in this space we have found ourselves

Philip Li

In this space we have found ourselves
I am having trouble finding more alcohol
To wipe down the boxes of food,
Make everything okay,
Quickly close the door before anything else gets inside,
And my hands, wash my hands, dry my hands,
Suck on my screen for a moment
Reminders that nothing will be okay
Or the same, or in agreement on the things we thought we knew to be true:
The online delivery windows; skip away, my shopping cart in shambles
No peanut butter, or masks, or toilet paper, or wipes.
Then the window vanishes and I load the cart up again with organic cereal.
By now the morning songbirds are dreaming.
Me, staring into the magic blue square, until exhaustion
Under the moon and clouds, Mother Nature smiles,
Always hope, under the constant lurking dread
The lack of wellness, the dying, the not caring, the
President, the stain.

Hanging onto hope for a better future, that keeps the slow
treasure we've gained, helps us learn from collective stupidity
Another day ends, and begins, and forgets.
Somewhere I hear a door close; someone whispers,
"I can't breathe, I can't breathe."

If I were the virus, I know who I'd get into first
And probably last as well, but we're too late for that.

I'm new, I'm kind of different, and I'm changing things
incredibly.
I am a price to pay, a blanket tax,
The return is a chance to see more clearly,
To be, something different than what was there before.
Success in excess in exchange for waste one cannot digest;
ignore it
Ambition to progress, balance be damned; ignore it
The need of more crushes the common good
And in this mad rush, a pause...

This hobbled system, focused on a future where so many
are left behind.
Trapped in a recurring and unexamined history
Tragic now because in the time granted you didn't care.

I don't have time
I don't have time
I don't have time!

But you have it now and still you can't find a way to
recognize each other
To love each other
Only to revisit the age old evils separating the tribes
Even in the pause
Already planning for its past tense
When the world opens and you feel strong again
You'll work so hard to forget what you can't control
Forget that there can be balance
A great claiming fire
Yet for the great majority of you, so angry at everything, so
scared and terrible, so dead inside

For you, my gift is ignored, your sickness is pure, rotting
you from the inside, and spreading, the stain of your
hatred, your ignorance, your cruelty, our hatred, our
ignorance, our cruelty
You will survive, just a hoax made by those against you
Those that think, that care, that ignore you.
And like that arsenal in your basement, you burn with
dangerous rage
Your antennae set to echo, your guns pointed at your
neighbor.

Hope.
Time you still have.
There is nowhere to go to, you have to breathe, take a knee,
together
Be mindful in the place and time, the environment of
reflection around you
Breathe,
Don't waste it.

Present

Kathryn Sadakierski

A birthday in the sun,
In the humid scent of summer
That comes with pool chlorine and cut grass.
A birthday in the sun,
Something magical in knowing
That you hold this special day,
This coming of age,
In your heart.

And the colors of the world metamorphose around you,
Everything changing in subtle brushstrokes
Even as we smell the same summer scents,
Hear the cars on the road past the trees, like normal,
Feeling the wind hustling past;
Everything is different,
But everything goes on.

Not everyone else knows
What this day is, or
The meaning of a ray of sun that is a benediction
Blessing your upturned face.
Nor do they realize the depths of the prism
That reflects back on the soul of a new day,
A year since last, another candle added to the cake.
Every motion of the day seems to you
Beautiful, a hope, a wish,
Because it takes place on this day.
In your heart, every fiber of life celebrates.

Dreams seem more possible,
Diffused across the earth

With the rippling kaleidoscopic span of butterflies' wings.
On your birthday, no happiness can be erased;
It is destined to be infused into everything
As you radiate your joy.
A birthday in the sun,
This year, not like any other one.

No quarantine can limit
The amount of love felt on this day,

Which isn't defined by things,

But by the peace felt in the present,

Which is made more meaningful with the clarity

Of what matters most, the wisdom to know

That this is everything, being born anew with hope.

The Way It Falls: Haiku During COVID-19

our thomas

pandemic
in the checkout line
first daffodils

home bound
days with no names
in spring

a friend
reported sick
i place my axe

checking again
that there is no fever
owl's call

stale crust
no news of illness
among sparrows

march winds
sadness of the woman
onscreen

quarantine
beetle crawls slowly
across a room

one petal
the way it falls
is uncertain

pandemic
thousands of stars
bitter cold

a dozen plums
no one to share them
but the moon

pandemic
empty purple dinosaur
in the wind

white clouds
robins mark time
the ordinary way

morning mist
where will we be
when it parts

week seven
my piss bubbles
form a raft

what we know
what we don't
mayfly sleeps

spring blasts
splitting pines
no vaccination

new normal
a line of ants
persists

A Silence Like No Other

Cynthia Sue Martell

Oh, I have known silence—
Not as a deaf person does,
or a widower's first night alone,
Nor that of a hermit monk who
seeks God as his only companion.

But never the silence of isolation
Plague so barbarously demands:
An ominous stealthy quietness
That subtly comes to possess both
Our exterior and interior worlds.

Very gradually a transition occurs—
A subtle appetite for silence evolves
One hungers for it especially at night,
With it comes an intellectual alertness,
Spiritual longing and intense curiosity

Short Stories

Wednesday's Child

Roy Sunter

Wireless Caller, the phone's display said.

Lisa set her coffee down with a sigh. *Wireless Caller* could be anyone. It was too early in the day for the usual barrage of robocalls, IRS impersonators, and dubious charities – but not for her neighbor, Cal. A widower at least 20 years her senior, Cal looked in on her regularly with an almost proprietary interest which she sometimes suspected was motivated by more than neighborly concern. But he never crossed the line into impropriety, and his eagerness to please her was only manifest by his willingness to tackle those home repairs she was unable to perform herself.

Or it could be her brother, Tony. Tony lived three towns away, and provided Lisa with periodic updates on their mother, whom they had been compelled to place into assisted living. Only ten minutes from the facility, he dropped in on her regularly – or had until the Plague had forced the banning of all non-essential visits. The prior week he'd broken to Lisa the news that the facility's walls had been breached – four of the staffers had tested positive – and that they lacked sufficient resources to test all the residents. Perhaps he was now calling with news to the contrary.

She let it ring twice more before answering. "Hello?"

"Morning, Lisa!" It was Cal. "Sorry to call you so early, but I thought you might want to know that Cameron's Market has toilet paper and bread."

Her morning lethargy fell away like snow sliding off a roof. "That's great news!" she said. "When did they get them?"

"Just last night," Cal said. "My boy supervises the night shift unloading the trucks. He just called to let me know. I'm headed over there right now – can I pick up anything for you?"

She hesitated for a moment. "Still limiting two per customer?"

"Probably. I didn't think to ask."

After a moment's thought she said, "Thanks, Cal, but don't worry about me. Grab whatever you need for yourself. I need a few extras anyway, I'll swing over there a little later."

"Okay, Lis. Not too much later, though. You know how it is."

"That I do. And Cal – thanks again."

After she disconnected, she sat for a moment before getting to her feet. Cal's call had turned what was to have been yet another predictably dreary day in quarantine into one whose outcome was uncertain. She was going to have to make an unscheduled trip Outside, and it wasn't even Wednesday, the day assigned her on the basis of her birth month. The assignments weren't strictly enforced – yet – but she dutifully followed the guidelines and restricted her resupply forays to Wednesdays. Now she was going to venture outside on a Monday. What were Mondays like, now? She remembered their rituals from before she was furloughed from her engineering job – the friendly greetings with her coworkers and staff, the bad coffee, the emails that had accumulated over the weekend. And what about those weekends? What had they been like? She barely remembered. One day now was pretty much like any other.

Except for Wednesdays. She knew well the Wednesday drill. One did not simply leave the house as in the old days, as if the outdoors were just an extension of the living room. There were preparations to be made, precautions to be taken. She knew to pack her handbag with at least one pair of impermeable gloves, at least one surgical mask, a small dispenser of sanitizer, and her state-issued ID.

Lately, she'd taken to slipping David's service pistol and her permit in there as well – just in case. One never knew these days.

She set the satchel on the desk, and from the bottom drawer withdrew the firearm. Certain odors seem to be forever linked with deep memories, and the smell of the leather holster never failed to evoke vivid recollections of him. At times she could almost hear his voice as he clumped up the steps from the entryway to the main hall; his contented groan as he collapsed into his favorite easy chair; and the mischievous way he sometimes called her "Liza" just because he knew it provoked her.

And as it usually did, the rest of it came back to her as well, like a persistent fever she couldn't shake. It was only supposed to have been a routine traffic stop – a carload of out-of-state college kids out joyriding. But a few days later the results of the mandatory testing at the end of his shift had been anything but routine. He'd not been allowed to return home, so she'd had to pack some personal items for him and drop them off at the hospital entrance. A week later the coup de grace arrived by telephone. It wasn't just the suddenness with which the Plague had claimed him - it was knowing that, in quarantine, he'd died alone.

Her last words to him had been, "Have a good day, Honey, see you tonight." She'd left the "I love you" unsaid, assuming there'd be more than enough time to say it later.

"Oh, David," she whispered, screwing her eyes shut to squeeze out the tears rather than waiting for them to fall on their own. There would be more than enough time later to shed a few more in remembrance. Right now there was work to be done, and a checklist for going Outside to be followed. She shook her head, exhaled, and returned her focus to the now. Uncharacteristically, this Monday had suddenly taken on a purpose, the promise of success precariously balanced against the likelihood of disappointment – with both outcomes occurring against a backdrop of risk. There was only one way to reduce the probabilities to certainty.

She removed the pistol from its holster and placed it into the purse. Then, after dressing and confirming that she had everything else she'd need, she shouldered the bag and stepped out into the combat zone the world had become.

Traffic was only a little heavier than usual, and she reached the store in short order. Since the parking lot was no more crowded than on a typical Wednesday, she wondered if perhaps word had not yet gotten around that scarce items were available. She donned her mask and gloves, quickly checked her hair in the mirror, and got out of the car.

A store employee serving as traffic monitor stood at the entrance, enforcing the limit on the number allowed inside at a time. She took her place behind a half-dozen or so people who had already queued up, silently waiting their turn to enter. The line moved relatively quickly, and before long she was inside, where a pair of store associates were disinfecting the carriage handless for the convenience of the customers. Their bored demeanor compelled her to wipe one down herself, including its rim, before setting out.

She pushed past the register lanes and followed the traffic arrows into the nearest aisle – health products. She hadn't planned on getting anything here, but she could always use another container of hand sanitizer. Even from where she stood, though, she could see its shelf location had been picked clean. She paused before a hand-written notice taped to the empty shelf urging customers to limit their purchases to two bottles. “Dammit,” she whispered. It had been a long shot, and her supply was adequate for her immediate needs; but there was no telling how long that supply would have to last. She continued to the end of the aisle, where she followed the arrows into the next – pet food and supplies, for which she had no need. But the aisle was adjacent the paper goods, and provided the quickest way to get there along the accepted traffic flow, so she quickly made her way past the bags of dog food and kitty litter, and rounded the corner at the end.

And here she felt as if she'd drawn a winning lottery ticket…

To her left, the racks stretched long and barren from one end to the other, with only a scattering of disposable dust cloths or damaged paper towel rolls punctuating the barrenness. But opposite those – El Dorado! The Emerald City! Identical packages of generic toilet paper, twelve rolls to a bundle! The display was far from full, but a stock boy was maneuvering a fresh pallet of tissue on a hand truck into position while another was ripping off its shrink-wrap. She stepped past them and grabbed a package as if afraid it would prove to be a mirage if she didn't, and dropped it into the cart, following it immediately with another. The nagging concern that she might be taking more than her share was eased by the fact that the two stock boys had already replaced the two she'd taken and then some.

Having gotten what she'd primarily come for, she felt an almost celebratory urge to buy some frivolous inessential to mark as special this bright moment in an otherwise dark time. She knew the gourmet foods were a few aisles away; and though she'd arrive at its No Entry end if she went there directly, the coffee aisle lay just beyond, where she could pick up a bag of her favorite roast. She proceeded to the paper aisle's exit eager to carry out this new plan – but found her way blocked by a pair of men entering against the arrows, each pushing a cart piled high with supplies.

They were dressed in hunting camo, their trouser legs loosely tucked into their boots, military style. One wore a black scarf over his face, the other a full face mask with glass eye ports and three HEPA filter housings over the nose and mouth. It was impossible to judge his age, but the one with the scarf might have been 18 or so. Each of their carts carried several cases of beer, and the maximum allowed number of various rationed items – institutional-sized boxes of pasta, an assortment of institutional-sized cans of beans and vegetables. Each of them now tossed a pair of tissue 12-packs atop their other spoils.

The one with the respirator nudged the other's upper arm with the back of his hand. "Leave some room, we still have to get meat." His voice was muffled, but he spoke loudly enough for her to make out the words. His younger companion nodded, and rearranged his cart's contents to more efficiently make use of its space. The older man looked around. "Goddamn it," he said, "Where the fuck is your mother?"

The other just shook his head and shrugged.

"Go find her," the older man said. "And tell her to get her ass over here while there's still TP. Leave your cart here, you'll move faster."

The youngster nodded again, and disappeared around the corner, abandoning his cart in the middle of the aisle. The man – his father, she assumed – rested his forearms on the handle of his own cart, partially supporting himself. He clasped his hands together and gazed vacantly down into its depths, as if in idle admiration of its contents, or as if he'd just switched himself into some kind of standby mode. Either way, he still partially blocked the aisle.

How thoughtless, she thought, though she was long past being surprised by boorish behavior. Times of crisis seemed to bring out the extremes of conduct at both ends of the spectrum. Unwilling to create a scene, she kept her aggravation in check. After all, she'd often forgotten to adhere to the one-way directive when it was first put into place. So she just cleared her throat and somewhat timidly said, "Excuse me?"

The man didn't look at her, but continued gazing towards the floor as if deep in thought.

"Excuse me, sir?" At this he looked up. She forced a smile. Pointing to the arrows taped to the floor tiles, she said, "I think you're going the wrong way..."

He stared at her for a few seconds, then down to where she pointed, then shook his head and looked away. He muttered something she didn't quite catch – it sounded a bit like "Good luck yourself, Trish" – though she was pretty sure that wasn't it. Her mild disapproval flared up into anger, but he stood at least a head taller, and probably outweighed her by 100 pounds. So she held her tongue, and gestured with her cart. "I wonder," she said, annoyed at the way her voice shook, "if I could just sneak by you?"

Without looking at her, he slid his cart far enough to one side for her to pass, which she did as quickly as she could without giving the appearance of flight. "Thank you so much!" she chirped. Bastard, she thought. "You have a nice day, sir, and Stay Safe!" She didn't stay long enough to see his reaction, preferring instead to imagine that her exaggerated show of neighborly good-will had thoroughly pissed him off.

She tried putting the encounter out of her mind, but it irritated her as persistently as an itch in the middle of her back. The Plague had seemed to provide a favorable niche for those who harbored a casual disregard for the needs of anyone but themselves. They took the otherwise sensible credo of self-sufficiency and anticipating the worst to an extreme, using it as an excuse to place their own wants ahead of everyone else's. She suspected their devotion to preparation went beyond material logistics, and included being prepared – and quite willing – to bully and intimidate those less aggressively selfish. It struck her as ironic that they seemed quite unaware that their hoarding was contributing to the very societal collapse which so alarmed them.

She wondered how the exchange might have played out had she produced David's 9mm, but dismissed the thought as nothing more than adolescent revenge fantasy.

Besides, she had toilet paper! Two dozen rolls! This called for celebration.

She wheeled past the exit of the gourmet section to the aisle just beyond it, coffee and tea. David had never cared for the flavored coffees, but since she'd been on her own she'd indulged her own fondness for hazelnut whenever she could. She cheerfully tossed a bag of her favorite brew into the cart and proceeded to the far end of the lane, where she doubled back to the entrance of the gourmet foods display.

The prices were a little daunting, but this was a special occasion. She found a jar of an exotic Middle Eastern spice blend she liked, and added it to her haul, along with a small bottle of perfumed cooking oil. She felt positively decadent and enormously pleased with herself as she made off with these extravagances.

She swung through the bakery for a fresh loaf of locally-baked bread, and finished with a tour of the dairy. She knew Cal was fond of imported bleu cheese, so she picked up a wedge for him. She owed him at least that much for alerting her to the store's restocked shelves. As an afterthought, she picked up a block of Parmesan for herself, and proceeded to the checkout.

Once outside, and pushing her cart towards her car, she saw the man in camo a few dozen yards away, placing his purchases into an SUV, while his son, and a woman whom she supposed to be his wife were doing the same. Because of the full-face mask he wore, it was hard to tell for sure, but she had the brief, disagreeable impression that he was looking her way, and had even paused in his task for a few seconds to watch her. Uneasily, she picked up her pace to her own car.

She was fishing around in her purse for the key when a man's voice nearby called, "Hey. You." Unsure whether or not it was meant for her, she looked up.

It was the man in camo, walking rapidly her way. It did not look like a friendly approach.

Her mouth went dry, and her heart felt like it had skipped a beat before revving up into a higher gear. "Yes?" she called back. "May I help you?"

He'd stopped about ten feet away. "Yeah," he said. The face gear masked his features and muffled his voice, but not the hostility. "I'd like to take a look in your cart."

She heard the words, parsed their meaning, but still couldn't make sense of the request. "What?" she said. "Why?"

"Because the goddamned store manager knew me and my boy were together," he said, gesturing back towards where his family stood by their SUV, "and they wouldn't let him buy any more TP or pasta. If my old lady hadn't gone through a different lane, we'd only have two lousy packages for the three of us!"

Her brain raced to keep pace with her mouth. "I – I'm sorry," she managed to say. "But what's that got to do with me?"

"You got two," he said, pointing to the toilet rolls. "And you're only one person. I seen you around, and I asked the cashier. She said you got no one at home. No husband, no kids. And since you gave me so much shit back there, I figured you owed me."

The scene was taking on a dark, surreal cast, ugly, nightmarish, and other-wordly. Nothing quite like this had ever happened to her before. With no reference point to guide her, no similar prior experiences she could use as templates to chart a course, she was at a loss for how to properly react. "Sorry," was all she could think to say. "I don't – I'm – I'm not sure I understand what's going on here."

"What's happening," the man said, "is that I don't think you need both of those, and you should give one of them to me." He took a few steps more and reached towards the cart.

She was so stunned by this turn of events that she just froze in a paralysis of disbelief. This was beyond anything she'd ever experienced. At least muggers have the sense to physically assault you first. And as she stood there dumbfounded, indignant, and more than a little frightened, her hand, still in her purse where it had been hunting for the key, happened to bump into David's pistol – and something in her snapped. Instinct took over for an intellect stalled with indecision, and she toggled from Flight to Fight. She backed up against her vehicle and closed her hand around the gun's handle. She withdrew it, adopted the two-handed grip David had shown her, and crouched. "No closer!" she heard herself say. "Back off!"

Visibly startled, the man stopped, dropping his arms at his side. For a few seconds they just eyed one another. Then he said, "You wouldn't. Not for a few rolls of bumwad."

She released the safety catch with an audible click. "No," she said. "Not for that. But to get rid of another asshole? You bet I would."

The confrontation continued in silence for a few more agonizing seconds. Then he slowly raised his arms. "Okay," he said. "Okay. Take it easy. I'm outta here." After he'd taken a few steps backwards, she straightened, but kept the gun leveled in his direction.

"Keep moving," she said.

He stared at her a few seconds longer, then slowly lowered his arms. He turned around and walked back to his vehicle without a backwards glance.

Her hands had begun trembling while re-engaging the safety and returning the weapon to her purse, and by the time she'd found the car keys, they were shaking so badly she could barely unlock the doors. She threw her purchases into the back, pushed the empty shopping cart to one side without returning it to the corral, and climbed in behind the wheel. She pulled the door shut, relocked all the entries, and burst into tears. Sobbing uncontrollably, she hammered her fists against the steering wheel in helpless rage.

What have we become? she thought. What have *I* become?

Change in the Air

Lynda Mabbs-Zeno

People are a skittish lot. I have heard that this is the result of evolution gifting Homo sapiens with a strong "fight or flight" response. I have tested this myself so I can confirm it is true. If I sneak up behind a woman and poke her in the back with a sudden, forceful movement of one of my digits, in a split second adrenalin will be flooding into her veins. Her heart rate will go up to ready her for an action which, in most women, will be to run away. Then just as she starts to turn around to identify what is causing this poking sensation, I bet every hair on her arms will suddenly stick up in the air in a defiance of gravity. She will probably scream, too. Yup, that is what happens.

This fear reaction can be so strong I can smell it on her like a perfume. In fact, I prefer the smell of fear to the bouquet of a perfume. The smell of perfume can be confusing to me. Am I supposed to enjoy the fact that a woman smells of fruits or flowers or something earthy that I might stumble across in the leaf litter of the woods? I would rather have my eyes be able to confirm the validity of what my nose has identified. I could take advantage of her fear if I had the inclination to do so. I could knock her to the ground before she becomes aware of what she is dealing with, but I usually don't bother adding this to my game. I figure that if I do nothing more than poke her, it is still going to take a good twenty minutes for her to calm down and that, in itself, is enough entertainment for me.

In my experience, I find that most men will react the same way to my sudden poke. However, there are some men who, in that same split second of the adrenalin rush, will feel fear and anger at the same time. That is not so good for me because being angry gives them a little confidence. They might start to turn around while also raising a fist to take a swing at my jaw. I can't sniff out in advance which men have the ability to react this way so I have to be on the ready for a possible retaliation. I used to look them over first in an attempt to assess whether they are tough guys, but that is a harder assessment to make these days as almost all of them are sporting tattoos. A brawl isn't my idea of entertainment. Well, maybe I am just getting too old for it.

I am a keen observer of people and I feel I am more intuitive about human behavior than most of them. This is probably because I spend a lot of time studying their habits and their responses to the goings on around them. Also, I don't over-think things. You can go overboard and miss the obvious if you spend too much time trying to psychoanalyze people. For me, scent detection plays a large role in my intuition, and right now my olfactory senses are frequently picking up the uneasy aroma of fear that is wafting in the air everywhere there are people. It is enough to give me nose fatigue. I have not been able to discern why fear would be on the rise. I don't see anything to account for it and I certainly haven't done any poking lately.

Now that the weather is warmer and I am spending a good deal of time outdoors, I have noticed some changes in the behavior of people. More people than ever are out and about, walking on the trails in the woods and along the neighborhood roads. I have been surprised to see so many people suddenly taking an interest in getting some healthy exercise outdoors. There are a lot of solitary walkers and, although sometimes I see a couple walking together, I rarely see more than two walkers together, and it seems that as strangers pass each other by they share unusually cautious glances. They may greet each other but it is usually with some feigned enthusiasm while they emanate that aroma of fear. What I haven't been seeing lately are the groups of teenagers who hike up the mountain to where there is a good view. I used to see a lot of them congregating in the parking lot at the trail head, laughing and jostling one another while they drink sodas. The parking lot at the lake, which usually hosts partying teenagers on warm summer nights, is always empty now. Maybe they are just busy doing other things. That's okay with me. I like ambling along in the early evening just as the sun is going down, and now I don't have to worry about stumbling across some inebriated football team captain who feels he has to display his top boy status in front of his friends.

Sometimes I walk along a wooded path behind a tall wall that runs alongside the highway. The dull roar of cars has always been an annoyance, but it is the wind that weighs me down, carrying with it the sounds and smells of the activities of the occupants in the cars. Warm days bring a cacophony of rap music blasting from open windows but, if I am lucky, I might also catch the odor of greasy hands trying to maneuver a steering wheel while cradling a Big Mac. That is one distraction that I actually enjoy. Recently, for some reason unknown to me, there seem to be less cars travelling on the highway. When a car does pass by it is not likely to deliver a treat for my olfactory senses, but will, instead, deliver the faint odor of fear.

My wooded path eventually comes to an abrupt end behind the buildings at a shopping center. The dumpsters there have always been an encouraging spot for rummaging around and, hopefully, finding discarded food, often in pristine condition. In the past I haven't encountered much competition for this bonanza of still-edibles. It was always worth putting in the effort required to take that long walk to the trash bins. However, on my recent trips the dumpsters have been empty, only satisfying my imagination with the sour odors of fats and sweets that still cling to the metal. I will make the trip a few more times to see if the situation changes, but if I keep coming up empty-handed, I will drop that route for a while as part of my weekly wanderings. Maybe I will check that spot again later in the year.

I am a creature of opportunity and I don't need much – just enough to get by. If the dumpsters remain empty, one option for me is to stroll over to the green lawns that surround the houses with showy patios and outdoor grills. I will quietly stand in the shadows of the big trees that edge the lawns. It will be a good test of my patience to stand there in silence, watching as meats are being roasted and flipped over. I will wait, and wait, and wait, until the meats are taken into the house. If I wait long enough, until the grates have cooled, I might be lucky enough to lick some tangy grease off the grill while those inside the house are preoccupied with happy chattering and the clinking of glasses. It is a bit troublesome, though, that this year, despite these warm evenings, I haven't encountered much in the way of patio cooking and inside chattering. When there is a breeze around the patios, it is not a breeze that carries sizzling sounds, fragrances of fat and distant laughter. It is only a silent breeze or one that carries the bird's song and the comforting rustle of leaves.

As I skulk around the shrubs closest to the house, I begin to get a whiff of that fear odor again. I don't know why this fear odor seems to be suspended in the air around people all the time now. It is an ominous aura. It is as if there is some invisible presence that is poking everyone. Of course, I am mildly curious as to the cause of the behavior changes I witness and the olfactory cloud of fear that hovers everywhere there are people, but I am, in general, indifferent to the problems of men. No matter what changes occur in the world of men, I will just continue to put my senses to good use. Right now the aroma of seeds is an enticement, especially when my other food options haven't panned out today. I will mount an attempt to take down some birdfeeders. The odds are that I will be successful. I always manage to get by.

Three Covid-19 Microfictions

Sarwar Morshed

1. Thus Spake the President of the Mortals

A vivacious girl was tested Covid-19 positive in a city. The authorities dutifully quarantined her family members and her boyfriend's.

So far so good. But it was just the tip of the iceberg. Contact tracing unlocked a whole Pandora's box - the girl had been maintaining a hexagonal relationship with four more clandestine Cupids in her fold! After conducting microscopic manhunt, the city administration put fifty star-crossed family members of the lover-quartet into quarantine.

This could have been the happy ending of the unusual love-lock impacted sufferings on fifty plus sacrificial lambs. But alas! This was not! One young officer of the local health administration with a degree in Statistics, created marks of anxiety on the foreheads of executives sitting on the upper-rungs of the officialdom. The seasoned statistician indulged in a permutation and combination game -

> "What if those golden extras of the girl have other girlfriends and those girlfriends in their turns have extra pro-active boyfriends ....?"

Taking the pragmaticity of the statistician's apprehension into cognizance, the President of the Mortals of that body issued his official verdict -

> "I do hereby command that the authorities be immediately asked to coerce the city-dwellers into complete quarantine until further notices are served."

2. The Wrong Call & Right Wife

I received a call, seemingly from my wife, this morning. She was crying profusely. I thought Covid-19 has injected strong doses of thanatophobia into her moral fabric. A metamorphosed version of her original self, she kept apologizing for her misbehaviour in the past. Sobbingly, she promised -

"I'll never be at cross with you, I swear. From now on, I pledge, I'll patiently listen to whatever you want to say. I'll certainly comply with your commands, my sweet sugar honey man."

These soft, sincere words, oozing with emotion and repentance from a termagant turned into a lachrymose lady, moistened my eyes.

I don't know whose significant other this gem was, as unfortunately, it was a call from a wrong number but surely she could have been the right wife for me!

3. The Palmist's Prophecy

Once, not long ago, a chiromancer, after deciphering the complex web of lines crisscrossing the landscape of my palm, predicted -

"A time will soon come in your life when you won't need to toil anymore - no commuting, no work, no office. You'll just regally cross your legs, relax at home, do facebooking, sit akimbo for yoga, relish your food and sleep at your sweet will."

What a charismatic Cheiro or Nostradamus I have found in the man! In the wake of the august advent of the Microbial Marco Polo, Covid-19, the government have imposed a countrywide lockdown and the promised times have befallen me so soon!

Grim Days for Dusty

Carl Mabbs-Zeno

The brand for Twisted Olive Branch Ranch was well known across the New Mexico Territory. It looked like a monogram of YOR but the Y represented the branch, not a letter. Dusty Graham's grandfather designed it more carefully than he designed the ranch itself, a rambling 150 square miles of rugged hills and high Chihuahuan desert along the Rio Chama which runs all year long when there are decent winter snows in the San Juan Mountains. His idea behind the brand was to stand close with a hand on his holster and ask direct of anyone contesting ownership of an animal to read the scar on the cattle's rump. And whether they could read or not, the answer was pretty much always "It's yor steer," and Dusty's grandfather would step back and smile and say "Damn pleased to hear we agree on that."

By the time Dusty took over the ranch, the controversies over land boundaries and water rights had been mostly settled. Cattle were contested but the brand was respected. Two generations of his family had expanded their holdings and maintained control of their water and the range with guns and guts along with astute, if rough, diplomacy with their Mexican, Indian and Anglo neighbors. Dusty knew it had come time for stability, for law and other institutions, for everyone to make money within the established boundaries. He had big plans and the will to see them through in the modern ways.

He hated any threat to his vision of stability. His sons were to be the first generation to get real schooling, live in peace, have some house servants; maybe one of them would run for some office in the territory government, be beloved of neighbors from all the cultures mingling in the beautiful, rugged wilderness where Dusty had spent all his years so far and, he expected, all the years remaining to him.

With such a clear vision of his legacy, he was short-tempered about the news from his oldest son on the first day of the 1890 round-up. The dust behind Hank as he rode toward the house showed from a good half mile off and showed he was riding too hard unless something bad was coming.

"What is it, son?"

Hank was not quite close enough yet to hear his father's words over the pounding of horse's hooves and his own heavy breath but he knew he better have something to say. He pulled back on the reins and slid to a stop.

"Somethin's killing 'em, Pa. We found a good 10, maybe 15, head dead just in the first morning. Lying in different places; none of 'em long gone neither."

"Well, what's doing it? They look sick or shot up or run over a cliff or what?" Dusty wanted to know everything right off.

"None of the hands can tell why they dying. Likely poison, we guess. What else could take a whole bunch that fast?"

"Got to be in the water but we only got good water 'round here. They around that trough on the north fork? If I was poisoning cattle, that's where I'd do it not to spoil the river."

"Oh yeah, that's where we started out this morning."

"Lemme get the big roan saddled up. We gotta look for tracks before they get too old. Go tell your mother I'm going out but don't say exactly why. Could be somethin' manageable."

By the time Dusty got to the trough, the hands had scouted around a lot more. There were some good trackers among them but no one came up with any sign. Some more dead animals were found and all of them were more or less near the trough.

As the sun was setting Dusty pulled Hank and some of the older hands together to plan what to do. He left out the younger sons, still in their teens, in case the talk got into some unsavory options.

"Heard anything about wanting to hurt the ol' Twisted Olive," he asked as he bit off a chew and handed the plug to the man beside him. The crew looked around at each other and murmured without distinct words but generally indicating no one had any ideas on that issue.

"Didn't think so. We're good neighbors. We got good neighbors. Not like in Grampa Graham's day. Maybe someone wanting to come in? Anybody heard of strangers in town? No? Thing like this not gonna be good for anyone. I ain't afraid of goin' back to those days if I hafta. I know how it's done. We got a strong hand, we know the land, we got good men and we care more about the Rio Chama than any stranger would. Hank and me'll talk to the ranchers here about. You Apaches pick one man to go talk to the tribe but don't rile them up. We ain't accusing. Ted, you get into Abiquiu and see if anyone's got ideas about taking land. Don't sound too worried. Sound like we're ready to handle whatever comes up. ...That's 'cause we are."

Dusty's hunch about a stranger fit right in with what Ted found and what the boys in the saloon were thinking best fit the facts. And the stranger recently come to town had no good reason to be there. No one comes to Abiquiu without roots or kin or invitation. He said he was studying geology and wildlife. Geology, they could believe but saying wildlife to study not even to hunt made no sense at all, particularly since people were saying the stranger looked to be from Asia. Ted figured he should take the

Chinaman out to the Twisted Olive Branch so Dusty could find out what he was about and yet he hesitated because of Dusty's modern concern for proper legalities. He hesitated for a couple more hours of discussing it with everyone at the saloon since they were paying for his drinks out of sympathy for his crisis and to repay him for bringing some real news into their tedious existence so by the time Ted went out to the stranger's camp, there was no one around.

It was two days after Hank's hard ride when Ted and the rest of the hands got together to tell what they found. Ted reported to Dusty that the town had run off the stranger and likely the problem was taken care of. The only other real news came from Adam and Able, the two younger sons, and the hands who stayed behind. More cattle were dying and two of the men were sick with some breathing thing.

"Awright," Dusty began after getting all the reports. "First off, nobody drink no water from 'round here. If there's nothin' getting sick in Abiquiu or Buena Vista, it's somethin' nearby. Hank, you ride back to the house and tell mother and then run down to town for good water. Maybe you go with 'im, Ted. Second thing we got to move the cattle. Bob Breakers up river from us and he hadn't any dead cattle so run 'em up there. I'll go up and warn him what we're doin'."

Dusty had acted quickly and decisively, like the leader of a good spread with sons who were set to lead the Territory someday not too far off. Moving the cattle out was a big job with them scattered across so much dry land.

When they gathered on Breakers' ranch nearly a week later, the toll on cattle was near a hundred dead and the toll on men was hard to say, except at least six were real sick. They had no way to test how many more were quiet sick and how many just exhausted.

When Bob Breakers' cattle started dying off, he rode with his whole crew down to Dusty's campsite. Breakers left his men mounted side by side and walked the last few yards to face Dusty. "You gotta get that herd back on your own land. They killin' my herd now. It's not much past breakfast yet. Be out before dark today, right?"

Dusty stood beside his horse and moved the rein to his left hand, not that he would pull a pistol on his friend but just to show he was choosing not to do something he could have done. "Bob, none of my animals been in with your herd. The trouble's in the water."

Breakers cut him off. "Maybe. I can't say what's killin' them but I can say you're gonna be gone before that sun is hits the mountaintops. We both know we gotta be good neighbors, but you know I mean that one way or 'nother."

This seemed fair to Dusty, about what he would have done himself if things were the other way around. Besides, it was looking like bad water was not the problem – sickness wouldn't be likely to move upriver. Still it was not his way and never would be his way to take orders. The two men stared at each other, not standing close but close enough that a twitch on either side could erupt into some nasty behavior that would not solve a thing. Dusty could see wrinkles across Breakers' face like his own, burned in and earned by fifty years of New Mexico sun and wind; could see Breakers' chest rising with a calm, slow breath; could see the tension in Breakers' riders poised to respond as one to a gesture from their boss. "It's your land," Dusty said with his chin pushed forward. In a single smooth movement, he swung around, slipped his foot into a stirrup and lifted onto the big roan. He waved his hand in a circle over his head to call his own hands together.

They'd all been watching and came quick. Breakers kept his boys lined up where they were. Like Dusty said, it was his land.

Dusty looked around, there weren't as many hands as there should have been. "Where's the rest?" he asked. No one answered. They understood the question. They didn't say they didn't know. They just didn't answer. Dusty turned to Hank. "Asked you a question, son."

"Two more too sick to work."

"Speak up, what else?"

"The Indians left last night."

"Why's that?"

"There was a lot of talk last night. We got eight men down now and some of them lookin' real poorly. And none of them's Indians. So I guess some men was thinkin' it's something caught from the Indians and the Indians was thinkin' it's better for them to be back on tribal land."

Dusty didn't see the sense of putting this on the Indians just because they weren't getting sick, but he needed and also knew the men needed to think they had figured out a way to stop the disease. So as soon as he got the herd back on his land, he went into Abiquiu to tell the town folk to send the Indians out from there too. It turned out, the folks in town were dying off faster than the ranchers, maybe because there weren't any older ones living out on the ranches. Also, they already decided it came from the Indians and ran them off. So it came down to what Doc Spencer could say and he was over in Buena Vista with his own town's troubles. With things looking worse in Abiquiu than back at the Twisted Olive, Dusty left out right away with Adam and Able. He had brought them along to get away from the ranch, a plan that had not worked out too well. They made it into Buena Vista shortly after dark.

The sheriff's office was empty. Dusty asked from inside the door of the Corona Saloon in the voice of a man that needs an answer, "Where's Doc Spencer?"

The barman waved him over. "We got a plague goin' here, you know? Doc ain't a real doc, you know. He tried but he can't do nothing for 'em. He's off to Albuquerque to get help."

"How bad's it here?"

"Three dead today. That makes 14 this week. Old ones, young ones only ones dying. We don't have many of them left. Indians musta brought it in, you know."

"The cattle dying 'round here?"

"Cattle? What they got to do with it?"

Doc Spencer came back two days later with the territorial medical officer, Captain Fauci, and a troop of soldiers. They set up a headquarters in the Sheriff's office. Right off the Captain stood on the steps and let a crowd gather to hear his speech. He wore a white coat which he didn't need to talk to a bunch of cowboys and townfolk, and a white hat he didn't need either but everyone wore a hat anyway. He said he couldn't cure anybody, but he knew what he had to do. Then he turned back inside. Dusty had to raise a ruckus to get in to see Fauci but Fauci was real pleased to talk once he met Dusty.

"Where you from?... When you first see it?... Where else you been looking?... How bad is it up that way?..."

Captain Fauci had a plan and his plan is what they did mainly because he had that troop of soldiers and had more brought in within a couple days. The local folk didn't like his plan one bit but it was the only one that made any sense at all. He said every soul had to stay within the area around five towns, counting in Coyote, Canones and Youngsville. He didn't post any along the Indian boundary but he sent a detachment to tell the Indians no one crosses that line either way. It was the strongest border wall of the quarantine.

Those five little towns with their shadows of cattle ranching survived past the six months of Fauci's law but they never grew much after that. You never heard of Abiquiu or Dusty Graham or the deaths in 1890 because Fauci's law kept it quiet. The white folks who lived through those times and lost their parents and their children left as soon as the soldiers were gone. The Indians never trusted the towns and ranches, and didn't go to them again for work or to live; just for trading. No one of any color wanted to move in until the memory of those days had dried up and blown away like the grand aspirations of Dusty for him and his boys. Adam and Hank had made it through. Dusty's wife was sick awhile and when she got better she went back east to a family she hardly remembered. Losing Able broke her more than the rest of the deaths, and the ranch and town business collapse combined. She lost her will but not until she got away from the Twisted Olive, and when she remembered what happened and told people back east about it, they shook their heads and felt sorry for her but they didn't learn a thing from it.

A Ventilator

Monica Raymond

You want me to take it outside and bring it in again through the other door? Do you know what a struggle I had getting it in through the revolving door? My brother just dropped me off at that little round area where you can't really park. This thing was propping up the trunk, he tied down the hood with one of his ties. He practically pushed me out the door, "Chandra, go, go, I gotta get to work...take it to her, come on, go..." He was late to work. You'd think he'd want to come in, see it really working on our mom, y'know. But that's not his way. White shirt, clean tie, flashing those pearly whites, pretend nothing's wrong. I don't think anyone at his workplace even knows our mom's here.

What is it? It's a ventilator. A ventilator for two. Two can use it at the same time, side by side. So if someone else's mom is in the next room, they can use it together. Very cozy. Like for sheesha! Just kidding. No, it's not FDA approved! My brother just finished building it. Don't look at me like that! It's not some rinky dink contraption he duct taped together in his basement; he's an engineer. He works at Pritzker. Something like this was his class project at MIT and one of the guys who he worked on it with messaged him that they should do it again.

So go out and come back in through that other door--why? It has a metal detector--so what? It's made of metal, so it'll go beep, beep, beep--very exciting, wake up somebody who's maybe sleeping for the first time in a couple of days. Come on, walk over here yourself, you can see it's metal. Yes, it could be a bomb. I suppose. But it's not a bomb, and even if the metal detector goes beep beep

beep making everybody crazy, that still doesn't make it a bomb. It's a ventilator.

It's experimental. Yes, I suppose you could say so. We spoke to her doctor. I can tell you don't believe me, but it's so. He said "Bring it in, we'll see." He knows the professor who advised my brother's team from some institute. Do you happen to know what time he gets in? Doctor Morrison? Usually around ten in the morning? That might be too late. I was here yesterday and she was having so much trouble breathing...and you know this little neck of the woods hospital doesn't even have one ventilator! Do you know that? It might not be FDA approved, but it's better than nothing. And probably a lot better--Sanjeev is very very smart! If I don't take it out and bring in through the metal detector you're going to call security? Oh God, why? Come. You can come over and look at it. I promise it's not going to blow anyone up. It's to save lives, not to...

Don't throw me out. I'm not going anywhere. I'm going to wait till Doctor Morrison comes in. I don't care when he comes--I'm going to wait. Or maybe--would you watch it? And I could go in and sit by my mom, and watch her breathe till he comes? I know it's early. But I heard this story. In New York, this man was on a ventilator, and everyone thought he would die. And somehow his wife got to stay with him in the middle of the night and she talked to him. For three hours. From three in the morning till dawn! And even though no one thought he would live, he did! He got better. I know it's very early. But go ahead. You watch it for me, for all of us, yes? And I'll go ahead and sit by her side, till the doctor comes.

Theater

Isolation

Dave Coleman

FADE IN:

INT. CARLA AND JAMES APARTMENT – DAY

Thirty somethings Carla and James sit in their tiny New York studio apartment.

Carla sits at a small desk and works on her laptop. James sits on the couch and thumbs through a gaming magazine.

James looks over at Carla -- waits for her to look at him. She knows it but ignores him.

JAMES
What ya working on?

CARLA
(after a beat)
I'm writing.

JAMES
Yea, what is it?

CARLA
(annoyed)
Short story.

JAMES
What's it called?

CARLA
Isolation.

JAMES
Isolation? Is your imagination on lockdown too?

James chuckles to himself.

CARLA
It's a working title.

JAMES
It must be working from home too.

Now James laughs out loud.

Carla keeps her eyes on her computer, the volume of her key strokes go up.

JAMES (cont'd)
What's it about.

CARLA
I'll tell you later.

JAMES
They say writers should share their ideas and if everybody likes the idea they should keep working on it, otherwise...

Carla, now really annoyed, shoots eye daggers at him and continues typing on her laptop.

With James still waiting, finally, she turns to look at him.

CARLA
(through a sigh)
It's a murder mystery.

JAMES
Oh really, what's the plot?

CARLA

A woman gets isolated with her annoying boyfriend and kills him.

JAMES
(after a beat)
Haha... Not very original. Plus, she'll get caught.

CARLA
Maybe she finds a unique way to kill him... makes it look like he caught the virus.

JAMES
Ummm, I don't think that's possible.

CARLA
Maybe she does research on symptoms and finds a combination of toxic herbs that mimics some of the symptoms, cough, headache, diarrhea, but slowly poisons him. Since she does all the shopping and cooking, he's clueless.

JAMES
I don't know. Kinda seems far-fetched. Yeah, doesn't really make sense. I don't think it's believable.

Carla does a quick search on her laptop and pulls up a page to show James.

JAMES (cont'd)
What's it called?

CARLA
Cardiospermumlasta. It comes from a plant in Africa.

JAMES
Uh, interesting, sounds real enough... but... Well, guess it's a good thing you're doing research for this story... I guess.

James picks up his magazine -- then sets it right back down.

JAMES (cont'd)

Still, why would she want to kill her boyfriend? I mean how annoying can he be?

She stops and looks at James.

CARLA

She was about to break up with him. She had been planning to tell him for months. She even booked two weeks in Monadnock.

JAMES

Oh, so he's not that bad -- it's just the situation.

CARLA

Maybe...

JAMES

Still working that part out?

Carla goes back to writing.

James goes back to reading. Then turns right back to Carla.

JAMES (cont'd)

What about her friends?

Carla tenses up, slowly but deliberately shuts her laptop.

CARLA

She didn't tell anyone okay. She didn't want anyone to tell him because, well, he's exceedingly annoying. Some might say pathologically annoying -- and she knew if he found out he would keep annoying her until she agreed to stay with him just to shut him up. So she kept everything bottled up inside, for months... until she JUST COULDN'T STAND IT ANYMORE.

James, stunned, just stares at her, surprised by Carla's burst of emotion.

After a beat, Carla bounces up and walks to their tiny kitchenette.

CARLA (cont'd)

You hungry? Got soup yesterday, I think you'll like it.

FADE TO BLACK.

The Amateur Astronomer's Analysis

-a radio play-

Carl Mabbs-Zeno

Sounds of TV coverage of a baseball game. A cell phone rings.

Robin: I hate waking up from a deep sleep to the clamor of a ringing telephone, especially when the first sensation from wakefulness is a sharp pain from my neck and across both shoulders, the heavy price of collapsing in front of the TV after dinner and drooping my head forward, stretching muscles that hate to stretch that way and dripping saliva from my gaping mouth. I also hate failing to answer the telephone since I am curious if a person, as opposed to a robot, has something to say to me. I allow one more ring to clear my head and bend my neck; the pain shoots down my back and fades as another ring sounds. I see the TV is showing a baseball game and I remember that it is a game from two years ago because the current season never began. Who can stay awake for a game two years old?...Uh... Hello.

Thomas: Hey Robin! I've got something for you!

Robin: Oh hi, Tommy. What's up?

Thomas: I just got a call from Al and then I went outside to see it for myself. There's something really bright and glowing in the sky to the northwest. You gotta see it. What do you think it is?

Robin: Hang on, fella, I'm going outside; just wait a minute. Northwest? I should see that from my front stoop.

The sound of the baseball game fades. A door opens and closes.
OK I'm outside now. Not northwest. It's really pretty close to exactly west.

Thomas: So you're seeing it now? What do you think?

Robin: Yeah, I'm looking at it. It's not moving so it's not a plane, obviously, or regular satellite. Too bright for a satellite anyway.

Thomas: You see the glow?

Robin: Yeah, I see that too, but I wonder if it's just the haze. Wait, no, I don't think so 'cause I can see the Pleaides behind it. They wouldn't be visible on a hazy night with a full moon like this. We have a full moon and that thing still stands out.

Thomas: What about Betelgeuse? Weren't you saying a while back that it was close to going supernova?

Robin: Yeah, it is. Not a bad guess on your part. I wish for that 'cause it would be the most spectacular thing we would ever see. But close to happening means it could happen sometime in the remaining lifetime of humanity. The chance of it happening in our particular lifetimes is miniscule.

Thomas: But possible, right?

Robin: Not in the middle of the Pleaides. Betelgeuse is Orion's shoulder. Long way off in the sky.

Thomas: Oh. You think it's a planet?

Robin: I wish I could say yes 'cause I don't believe in anything too strange, but no, it's too bright to be a planet. I look at Jupiter's moons and Saturn's rings through my telescope on dark nights sometimes so I'm used to seeing the big planets. This is way brighter than Mars too. Hang on and I'll set up the telescope – it's right here in the hall closet. Or do you want me to call you back?

Thomas: I can stay on the line. I want to know what you see. I told Al you have a 'scope.
A door opens. There is clatter of rummaging in the closet.

Robin: It's a cheap one I scavenged from a couple broken ones dropped off at the recycling center.

Thomas: Better than anything I've got.
The closet door closes, then the house door opens and closes. Footsteps cross the porch and go down some stairs.

Robin: OK, I'm setting it up. Got to pick up the thing... Hang on... Takes a minute to find it... There! Let me focus.

Thomas: You see anything?

Robin: Oh yeah! Damn, this is way cool! Oh yeah, I can see it now. It's not round! It's kinda U-shaped.
The door opens.

Teenage Son: Dad, who you talkin' to?

Robin: I'm on the phone with Tom. We're looking at that light over the driveway.

Thomas: Your boy come out?

Robin: Yeah, he's here too. Tell you what I think – I've got a few ideas. It's not moving so it's either really, really bright and a long ways off or it's a geosynchronous satellite. In the west at 9 pm, it can catch the sunlight and be bright like that if it's huge, maybe, or very low. So I'm guessing low...

Teenage Son: Lemme look!

Robin: Come on, take a look but don't bump into the scope. If you move it, it's hard to get it back in place...

Thomas: So is this like the lowest satellite ever? Why's it so bright? I never saw one like this before.

Robin: No, I never did either. And I never saw one with a shape I could see in the 'scope. I saw the Mir, the space station. It is not round but it was just a bright dot in my 'scope. And, of course, it was moving.

Teenage Son: Oh, man, Dad! I see it. Glowing with a scoop shape!

Robin: Did you hear that, Tommy? I have confirmation from another set of eyes that it is not round... Okay. Let me look again now.

Thomas: You like any of your own ideas?

Robin: Wait a minute... I need to get it back in the middle of the field. I've got more ideas. Elon Musk has started putting up a thousand satellites in geosynchronous orbit. Could be one of his in a really low orbit for testing purposes. If it's low, I might be able to pick up the shape of it.

Thomas: And it would be U-shaped?

Robin: Not that I know of but it might not be round. And in my 'scope I can't see it exactly. But there's another possibility – could be some kind of public art. Caught your eye, didn't it? Apparently sending up satellites is getting cheaper. I heard of a proposal a couple years ago to put up an artificial moon to make the night brighter. Wouldn't need so many parking lot lights, I guess.

Thomas: This isn't that bright.

Robin: Yeah, I didn't mean to say it was the same project... just that there are some weird projects out there.

Teenage Son: Listen to this, Dad! You want weird? It's all over the internet; trending like crazy. You remember Oumuamua?

Robin: What? We're talking about this bright light, not your teenage celebrities.

Thomas: What? I can't hear you right.

Robin: My boy's distracted by something on the internet.

Teenage Son: That's okay, I didn't remember the name either. It was something that came from outside the solar system in 2017. Remember that? The first interstellar traveler?

Robin: Oh yeah, I do remember that. Cigar-shaped rock, right?

Teenage Son: Says here that was never really known, what it was. It went by too fast; we saw it too late. Says here this thing you're looking at came from interstellar space too. The astronomers saw it coming. They were ready this time and they saw it slow down and settle in.

Robin: Did you overhear that, Tommy? My son found someone on the internet claiming it's a space ship.

Thomas: I hear you. That's better than a supernova.

Teenage Son: Not just someone. The report comes from the Arizona Institute for Astronomy. It's got Nobel Prize winners on its staff. And every other astronomy authority is weighing in now. Their tweets are popping up all over.

Robin: Tweets? That your source?"

Teenage Son: Dad, listen to the science. This is not some old black-and-white movie. Says here they've watched it approach and watched it orbit us for a couple months. The scientists stuck together- they waited to understand it better before making an announcement. Now that it has moved closer to earth, they're speaking out.

Robin: You're saying legitimate academics are reporting this is an alien craft?

Teenage Son: That's right. I don't like it but that's who's saying this. Hold on, here's a new article. It's from one of the observatories on a mountain in Hawaii. Says they sent up a probe a couple days ago. That may be why it moved closer to earth. They knew we'd found 'em.

Tommy: *unintelligible*

Robin: Sorry, Tommy, I can't hear you with my boy getting all operatic about what he's reading from his phone. Take a look yourself on the internet. If there is anything to this rumor..."

Teenage Son: It's not a rumor. It's from real scientists, lots of them.

Robin: ...it'll be easy to find. Gotta be on CNN, at least...
Sound of footsteps up to and across the porch.
I'm going inside to see what's on TV.
Sound of door opening and closing.
Talk to you tomorrow unless this has some truth to it in which case there may be no tomorrow.
Sound of door opening and closing again.

Teenage Son: You just think it can't be true 'cause I found it or 'cause it's on Twitter? That's the way news gets out fastest. Don't you want to know now what it's doing? Wait... The observatory spokesman is saying the craft is like a big glass banana. They've some good shots of it from the probe, not close-up but pretty good. It's just like Oumuamua: same size, same shape, came from the same direction, everything.

Robin: Thought the first one was shaped like a cigar?

Teenage Son: Sorta like a cigar, but now there're saying it was more like a bent cigar... And, oh no, it shot a payload to earth back in January. It looked like a banana shape to me, Dad. Didn't you see the same thing?

Robin: Yeah, I guess. Let's turn on the TV and see if this story is running on every channel.
Teenage Son: Whoa! They could tell the package landed in China, in Wuhan! They're saying they musta sent the corona virus! Makes sense. When you travel through interstellar space, you can't bring big weapons. A spoonful of virus could wipe out the only species capable of giving invaders a hard time.

Robin: Slow down, Son. Take a few breaths...

Teenage Son: What do you mean? We can't just relax because you haven't seen it on CNN yet. This is the biggest thing ever to happen on earth! I just hope we can survive it! Or maybe the corona virus cure is good for us after the initial shock, maybe it makes us smarter or strong or something. Maybe it's pure evil but we can fight it! For sure we've gotta do what we can and fast. I'm getting Mom.

Robin: I'm getting Mom up too. She's sleeping on the couch. See, there's a movie on now, not a panicky reporter from Orson Welles. Oh damn, the President's on CNN! And it's 9:30 at night!

Teenage Son: See? Listen to it.

President Trump: I will say it again before I give the microphone to Dr. Brian Luzon, Scientific Director of the Naval Observatory here in Washington and then we will have Neil Degrasse Tyson on video from his home in New York..."

Teenage Son: See? This is the big one!

Mother: What are you watching? Why do you have to make so much noise? I was sleeping?

Teenage Son: You'll want to see this. It's not some movie, Mom; it's for real!

President Trump: That's right isn't it? We'll have Neil in a few minutes, right? OK, let's get this Luzon up here. Come on up. Speak into all these mics. He's going to explain all this about an alien invasion is fake. All right, some people are meaning well, but there's no invasion and if there was we could have handled it anyway. We have options, lots of them. I mean we wouldn't go out and shoot a pistol into the sky. We have some really nasty weapons when we want to use them.

Robin: Oh no! I think you may be right, son. There may be an alien dropping virus on us.

President Trump: They're saying these aliens are much smaller than us. Really tiny, you know. There are enough on that one ship to take over the earth. But no, they're wrong. There's no ship. And if they were small enough to fit some huge number of them on board, they wouldn't have brains big enough to compete with us. I mean, look at how much power there is in the human brain, very powerful, especially certain ones that have proven themselves with success in many things.

Luzon: Thank you Mr. President...

President Trump: Just a minute Luzone, no Tucson...

Luzon: Luzon

President Trump: Okay Luzon and I'm still the President, you know. I get to say my piece first and as long as I want. I was just saying people should stop worrying about this. You already made your report to me, right? It's all under control. I immediately had the best people look into it and I'm telling you I know this is all a hoax. I don't know who started it, but I will know, and soon. We will figure out who did this. I'm thinking it may have come from China, you know, so they can blame someone for the virus they started. Maybe not. Maybe it wasn't them but that would make sense, wouldn't it? We'll know very, very soon. But first, let's hear from our scientist. OK, Dr. Luzon, you're on. First tell us about all your degrees as a scientist. We have the best here. You're one of them.

Luzon: Thank you Mr. President. As the President had stated perfectly clearly, there is no alien invasion and the corona virus did not come from outer space. We have no doubt at all about this. That light some of you can see in the west is very well known to astronomers including amateurs. Look on any website with descriptions of the April night sky or any current astronomy magazine. The brightest object in the night after the moon, especially soon after sunset or soon before sunrise, depending on the time of year, is Venus. Venus is in the western sky right now, in front of the Pleiades. It is in a crescent phase, visible through strong binoculars or almost any telescope set on a tripod. Furthermore, the shape is exactly what we know it would be at this time. Venus has phases like the moon. They depend on the relative location of the sun, the earth and Venus.

Teenage Son: Oh man! Is that boring!

The sound of the television fades to background.

Mother: What's going on? Why is Trump addressing us at 9 o'clock from his desk in the Oval Office?

Robin: Didn't you want the earth to survive?

Teenage Son: They weren't going to destroy earth, just humans. Besides, Trump says we could've stopped them.

Robin: Just the humans. Much better. And so much safer to know Trump has promised to use the best and biggest weapons.

Mother: Whatever are you talking about?

Robin: Nothing. A whole lot of nuttin'. Venus scared some folks. Starting with Al and then Tommy.

Mother: Venus who? What'd she do?

Teenage Son: Looks like that link to the Hawaiian observatory might have been fake.

Mother: Isn't that Neil Degrasse Tyson? Does he know this Venus? It must have something to do with astronomy. Turn up the sound.

Robin: I'll get it. What channel was that movie? It just started at ten, right?

Teenage Son: You gonna call Tommy back? Explain it? Tell him to tune in to the President?

Robin: He'll figure it out. Grab me a beer, willya?

THE AUTHORS

Mona Anderson, now retired, worked for 23 years in the Counseling Center at Keene State College as a Clinical Mental Health Counselor, Sexual Violence Prevention Coordinator, and Assistant Director. She and her husband, Joe Kohler, have lived in Alstead since 1979.

William Bryk, a retired lawyer, wrote columns for *New York Press* (1998-2003) and *The New York Sun* (2003-2005). He writes non-fiction essays on local history and eccentric characters, and an occasional memoir. Since 2016 he's contributed to *Splice Today, The Daily Beast, The Mud Chronicles,* and *The Limrik.*

Amanda Burns is a writer and teacher who refuses to move more than 15 miles from the beach. Though writing is her first joy. She spends most of her time teaching preschoolers how to engage beautifully in the world around them, a different type of art form.

Cai Ying Ming, is now a junior at Hainan Normal University. Her poems have been widely published in China and internationally. She was shortlisted for *the 4th China Young Poet Award* in 2019 and *the top 10 Chinese Poets of the Year* in 2019. She published her first poetry anthology *Name* at 20 years old.

Valerie A. Carter moved to New Hampshire two years ago with her husband, Greg, her son, Zachary, and their four-legged family members. She writes mostly nonfiction and is currently working on a memoir. When not reading or writing she might be found enjoying nature, theater, music, gardening, cooking, conversing, laughing, or napping.

Bill Chatfield is the founder and director of Peterborough Poetry Project, which promotes poetry in Peterborough and beyond with the vigorous help of the 5-member board. He has published poems in *Spectrum Literary Arts Magazine* (NU), *The Mud Chronicles* (Monadnock Writers' Group), and *Word Daubers* (ROMP).

Chen Yihai was born in Dongtai, Jiangsu Province. Educated at Soochow University, Ph.d in comparative literature, 2002. Professor and Dean of the Department of Social Studies, Yancheng Teachers University (YCTU). Member of Chinese Writers Association. Chairman of the Association of Critics of Yancheng. He lives in Yancheng, Jiangsu Province.

Dave Coleman is the President of the Piinch Company, a digital marketing company. Writing has always been a passion, but with not ever feeling comfortable with his command of the written word, he returned to school in 2012 and received his master's in English in 2014 from Southern New Hampshire University.

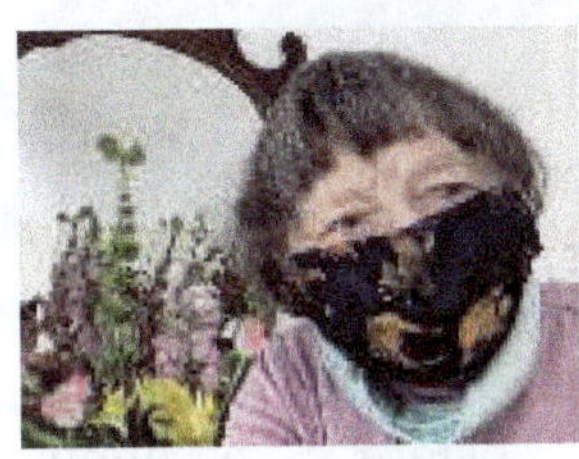

Ann B. Day writes poetry and is a photojournalist and nature columnist for several papers and magazines. She operated a farm in Mad River Valley VT for 60 years with her family until she moved to RiverMead in Peterborough, NH in 2013. Nature and the outside world is where you find Ann.

Julie A. Dickson is a NH poet whose works range from current events to environment, animals, nature, teen issues and memories. Her poetry has appeared in Ekphrastic Review, Blue Heron Review and Harvard Press, among others. She was nominated in 2018 for a Push Cart Prize. Dickson is active in PSNH and other NH poetry groups. She makes her home in Exeter with two rescued cats.

William Doreski has published three critical studies and several collections of poetry. His work has appeared in many print and online journals. He has taught at Emerson College, Goddard College, Boston University, and Keene State College. His most recent books are *Water Music* and *Train to Providence*.

Pamela Erdmann moved to the Monadnock Region in 1974. She attended Antioch, and worked at Monadnock Family Services in Peterborough before becoming Associate Chair of the Counseling Psychology Department at Antioch. She then began teaching Mindfulness at University of Massachusetts, in Mass Hospital and in the Massachusetts and New Hampshire prison systems. She is eighty-three years of age and looking for the next adventure.

M. D. Flyn is a voracious reader, a writer, and a chocolate inhaler. She is a lover of all things fantasy, scifi, and otherwise weird. A goth cheerleader for the little guy, she aspires to be your geek mom. You can visit at her blog MDFlyn.com or Twitter @mdflynwriter.

Sarah Franklin is a retired choreographer, dancer and teacher. She lives in Keene, NH, where she dabbles in movement exploration, jewelry making, gardening and writing. She has given a Tedx presentation, is very involved in community organization and lives part-time in France with her husband Michael. She is grateful to be part of this anthology.

Jess Gerrior is a gardener, environmental educator, and Doctoral Candidate. She has taught in sustainability, life sciences, and food studies, and is currently writing autoethnographic research on experiences with food systems while working with nonprofit and community-led efforts to build local food resilience. She lives with her tribe in Antrim, NH.

Claire Mowbray Golding is a freelance writer and editor. She was the 2003 recipient of the Worcester County Poetry Association's Frank O'Hara Prize, and has published a chapbook, *Poems and Other Offerings*. She has been nominated for a Pushcart Prize and lives in Princeton, Massachusetts.

Irene Kreissle writes from Keene, NH. She cherishes her husband, her mother, her basset hound and her kitty.

Larry Lefkowitz has had over 150 short stories published in journals, anthologies and online. His story collection "Enigmatic Tales" is published by Fomite Press. He is at work on a humorous literary novel.

Philip Li is a husband and a father, lives and works outside of Washington, DC. He's a worried parent, decent baker, mindful runner, global citizen, reader, watcher, listener. This is his first writing submission in a long time and he's very happy to have done it.

Denise Linnay challenged herself in March 2020 to write a poem a day as a way of keeping hope alive when she found herself in a full-time caregiver situation that increased her level of stress and isolation created by the COVID-19 pandemic. Her sixty-nine poems in sixty-six days were the therapy she needed to thrive. Denise lives in Ottawa, Ontario, Canada; she began writing creatively in 2015.

Carl Mabbs-Zeno retired in 2015, following many years as a U.S. government economist working on foreign aid. Since then he has published four novels and given up on a couple others. He and his wife, Lynda, live in and enjoy Peterborough, New Hampshire.

After retiring from a career as a horticulturalist and landscape designer, **Lynda Mabbs-Zeno** became a caregiver to her mother. The COVID crisis has forced her to end daily visits to the facility where her mother resides. She hopes now she will be able to spend time with her mother again someday.

Maura MacNeil is the author of the poetry collections: *A History of Water*, *Lost Houses*, and *This Last Place*. Her writing has been published and anthologized in numerous publications including: *Poet Showcase: An Anthology of New Hampshire Poets; Voices from the Robert Frost Place Volume II; On Our Own; Shadow and Light: An Anthology of Memory* and *The Mud Chronicles: A New England Anthology.*

Cynthia Sue Martell is a 4th generation New Hampshire native. For over two decades she and her husband operated Sunnyfield Farm in Peterborough, raising internationally recognized Jersey and Hereford Cattle. Cynthia now lives in a log house on the farm's 'back-forty'. This location provides her with the blessings of solitude and natural beauty, which nurture her poems, short stories and essays.

Rodger Martin's work has been published in literary journals and anthologies throughout the United States and China where he also wrote a series of essays on American poetry for *The Yangtze River Journal.* He is a New Hampshire State Council on the Arts in Education roster artist and a touring artist for the New England States Touring Foundation administered by the New England Foundation for the Arts. He has also received an *Appalachia* award for poetry, a New Hampshire State Council on the Arts award for fiction, fellowships from The National Endowment for the Humanities to study T.S. Eliot and Thomas Hardy at Oxford University and John Milton at Duquesne University.

Sarwar Morshed is a Professor of English at the University of Chittagong, Bangladesh. His works have appeared, among others, in *The Bosphorus Review of Books, The Bombay Literary Magazine, City: Journal of South Asian Literature, Star Literature & Reviews, Contemporary Literary Review India, Arts & Letters* and *the Ashvamegh*.

our thomas is a poet and artist working in Exeter, NH, where he lives with his wife, daughter and dog. He counts birds, Japanese gardens, and the woods among his interests and inspirations. He sometimes posts his work at <ourthomasart.com>.

The poetry of **Pravat Kumar Padhy** has received many awards and commendations including the Editors' Choice Award at Writers Guild of India, and the Kloštar Ivanić International Haiku Award. His Japanese short form of poetry has been widely published and anthologized. He has seven poetry books to his credit.

M. S. Munro (pen name of M. Susan Patterson) is a fairly new resident of Jaffrey NH, having taught literature and writing for 25 years in Texas, Mexico, Egypt, and China. Susan has published a book of poetry, a personal development book, curricula, and various articles for education and literature. Currently, she writes copy and blogs for small business clients, as well as her own blog.

Monica Raymond writes poems, plays, librettos, lyrics and sometimes prose from an old house in Cambridge, Massachusetts. A MacDowell Colony Fellow, Massachusetts Cultural Council Fellow, Swan Fellow (Vermont Studio Center), and Playwrights' Center Jerome Fellow, Raymond has taught writing and interdisciplinary arts at Harvard, CUNY, and the Boston Museum School.

Elaine Reardon is a writer and herbalist. Her first chapbook, The Heart is a Nursery for Hope, won first honors from Flutter Press in 2016. Her poetry has been published by UCLA Journal, Naugatuck Review, North Dakota Quarterly, Henniker Review, Smokey Quartz, New England Memories, and similar journals. She's been a feature in Dublin Ireland radio and local television, and she was recently nominated for the Push Cart Prize.

Roxanne Rubell is a freelance journalist who has written myriad feature articles for a diverse range of print and online media outlets including Spin.com, the NH Union Leader and American Art Review. She's currently working on a collection of personal essays and a new series of abstract paintings while working as a PR/Marketing consultant.

Kathryn Sadakierski is a 21-year-old graduate student whose writing has appeared in *Critical Read*, *NewPages Blog*, *Teachers of Vision*, *The Ekphrastic Review*, *The Voices Project*, and elsewhere. She graduated summa cum laude with her B.A. from Bay Path University, and is currently pursuing her Master's degree.

Stephen Seraichick lives in Keene, New Hampshire, and is married with two adult children. This fall will be his thirtieth year as an educator. He has written poetry since the late 60's. He was intrigued by the works of Lawrence Ferrlinghetti, Gary Snyder, Richard Brautigan, Maxine Kumin, and Anne Sexton. Currently, his favorite poet is Ellen Bass.

Barbara Snow: Recently retired from too many years working in the financial services industry, Barb was busy pursuing her bucket list travel goals before the virus shut everything down. Playwright, fiction writer, working on a memoir, and hoping for a vaccine real soon.

Except for four years at UNH, **Roy Sunter** has lived his entire life since age 11 in the Monadnock region. He is now a retired engineering physicist living on a dirt road in Fitzwilliam, where he dabbles in photography, mathematics, computer programming, writing, audio recording, and day hiking, as his whims dictate.

M. Allyson Szabo began writing in her early teens, inspired by authors such as Piers Anthony and Robert A. Heinlein. Her family encourages her, and supports her in her writing. She spends her weekdays writing. Weekends, you can find her at assorted Renaissance Faires throughout New England.

With over 25 years of voluntary sector experience, **Jennifer E. Tirrell** has worked alongside many wonderful individuals serving the underserved across the United States and beyond, as well as numerous community organizations. She loves to write and has hosted and encouraged groups in her home and community.

Volkert Volkersz is a songwriter, composer, and storyteller, who currently edits the weekly "Hubbub" newsletter for the Dublin Community Center. Born in Amsterdam, raised in Seattle, he lived and worked in Washington State as a music teacher and school librarian until retirement in 2016. He now lives in Peterborough, his wife's hometown.

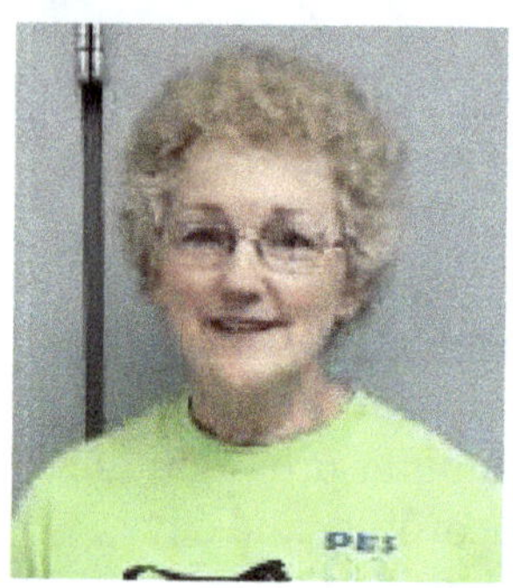

Patricia Zube has been published in Northern Essex Community College chapbooks and has received the winning adult entry for two years. As an elementary school teacher, she developed and ran the after-school poetry club. She is a member of the Poetry Society of New Hampshire, SCBWI, and The New Hampshire Writers' Project.

The Monadnock Writers' Group

Established in 1984, the primary mission of the Monadnock Writers' Group (MWG) is to offer fellowship and support to professional writers and to those actively engaged in developing their writing skills.

PO Box 3071
Peterborough, NH 03458

http://www.monadnockwriters.org/
https://www.facebook.com/groups/monadnockwriters/

Penning the Pandemic is the eighth printed anthology produced by MWG. Copies are available from MWG for:

The Mud Chronicles – 2018
Shadow and Light – 2011
The Monadnock Reader - 1990

MWG also produces *Smoky Quartz, an* online journal of literature and art.

https://monadnockwriters.org/publications-2/smoky-quartz-online-journal/

www.ingramcontent.com/pod-product-compliance
Lightning Source LLC
Chambersburg PA
CBHW071517100726
47908CB00004B/1200

* 9 7 8 1 7 3 3 1 2 6 2 5 0 *